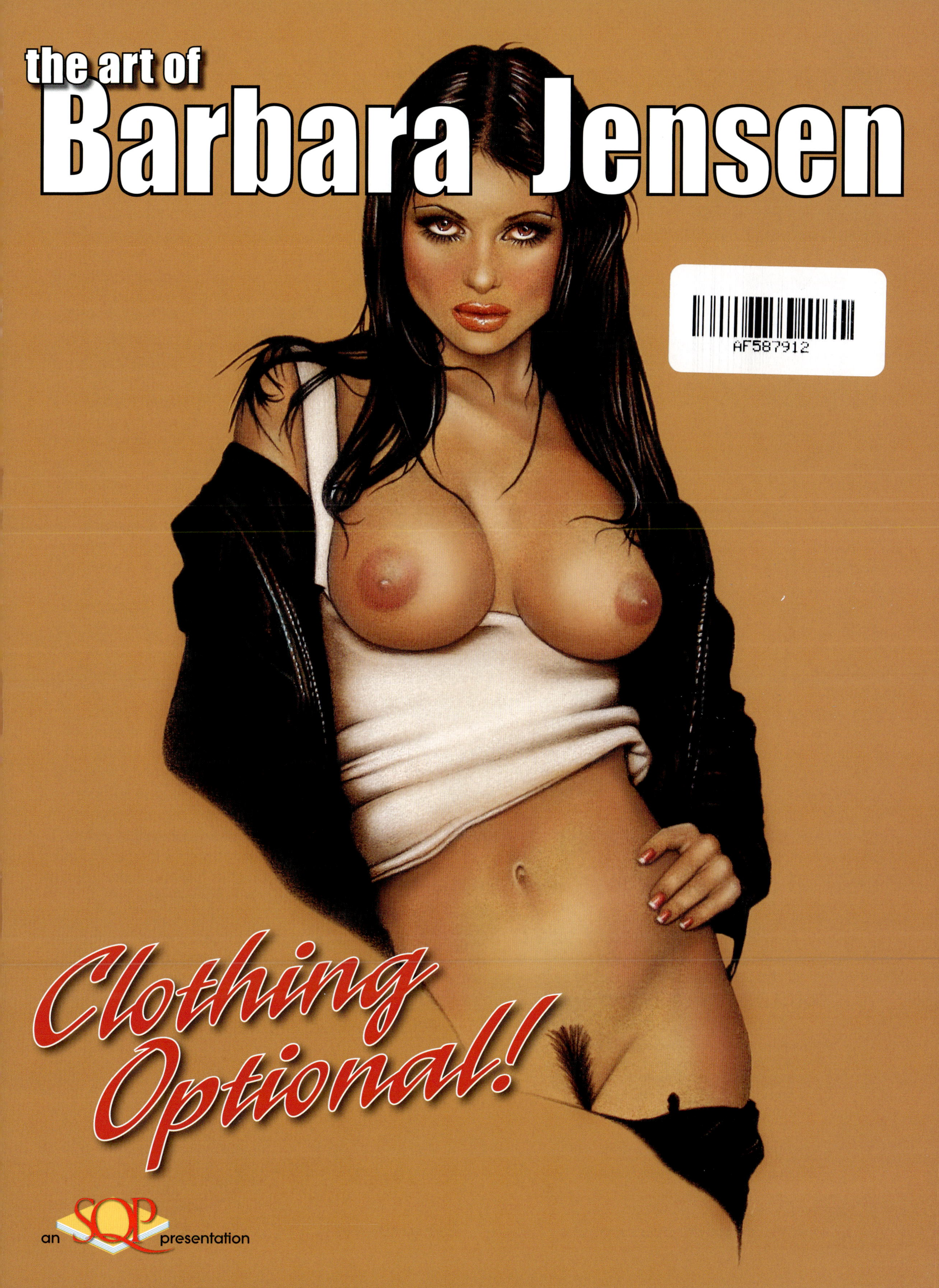
the art of
Barbara Jensen
Clothing Optional!
an SQP presentation

Broad Strokes

The Art of Being Barbara Jensen

Barbara Jensen was born and raised in Westchester, New York and now resides in Daytona Beach, Florida. As a youngster, she enjoyed sketching monsters, horses, and Barbie dolls (tellingly, both clothed and unclothed!) Those sketches and doodles eventually grew into a serious interest, and she would often raid local bookstores for instructional tomes on illustration and art techniques.

Aside from a few college art classes, Barbara is a self-taught success. By the late 90's she had progressed from straight-up portrait work into full-on erotic illustrations. A lover of the airbrush style (but admittedly mystified by its actual application), Ms Jensen developed her own unique "faux-brush" with an imaginative combination of colored pencils, charcoals, pastels, acrylics, and ink.

Being a female artist in a fairly male world of pin-up and erotica, Barbara also has a unique style when it comes to rendering her subjects. Effectively taking a "man's perspective" of what he wants to see, with her own personal sense of how a woman wants to be seen. The melding of the two directions provides a remarkable fully realized piece of artwork. Using both live models and photo reference, that delightful spark she creates is also guaranteed to be exquisitely detailed and rendered. Intimacy plus precision is her hallmark.

Ms Jensen's work can be found in art galleries, on book and magazine covers, and even on the labels of some high-end wine bottles! Her greatest love is still doing commissions for clients, fulfilling their wildest fantasies...on canvas that is!

You can find her prints and galleries at **www.Eroticartistgallery.com** and for the psp graphics world her tubes can be found at **www.Barbarajensentubes.com**

Always feel free to write to her concerning commissions at **Arteest111@aol.com**

The Art of Barbara Jensen
Clothing Optional!

Book design by Grassy Knoll Studios.

Published by SQP Inc.
PO Box 248 - Columbus NJ 08022

Sal Quartuccio & Bob Keenan - Publishers

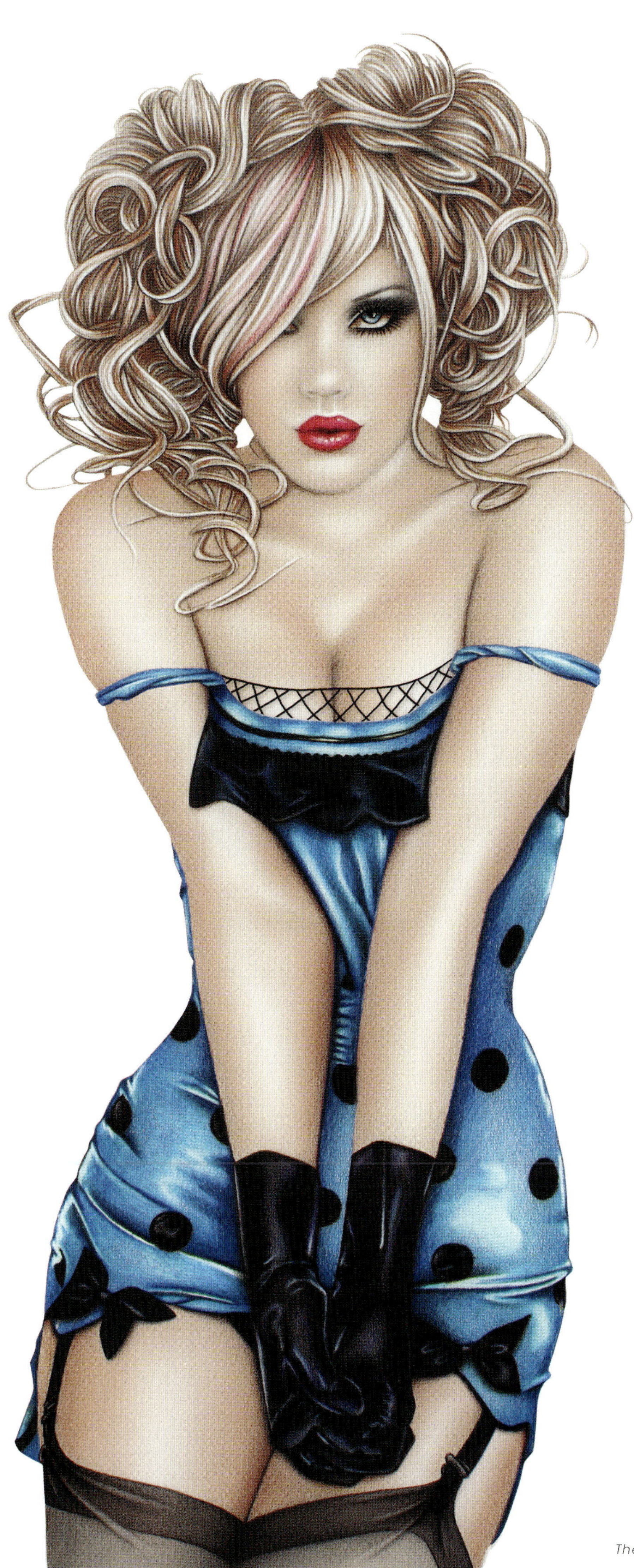

Burlesque Blue

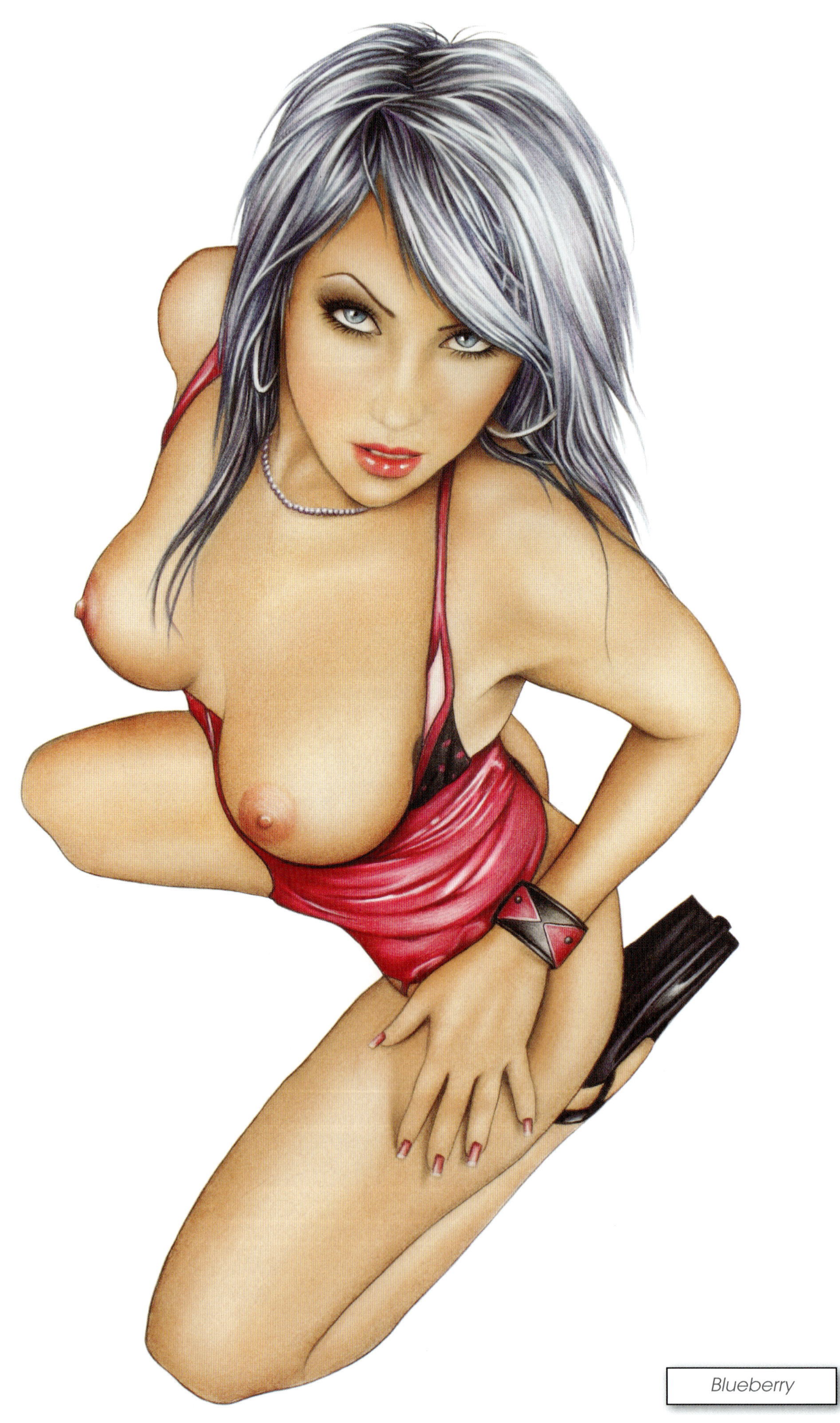

Blueberry

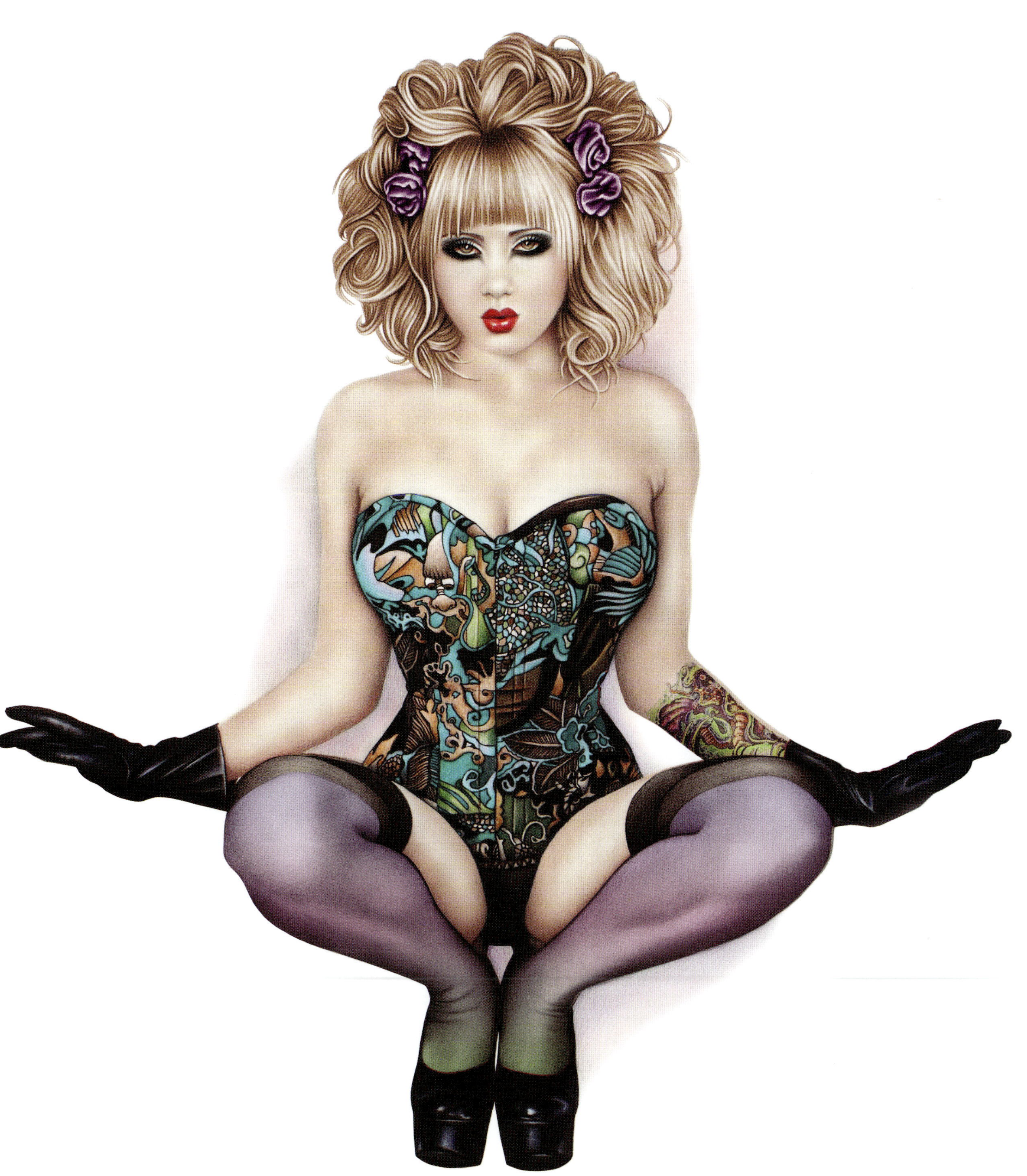

Clash

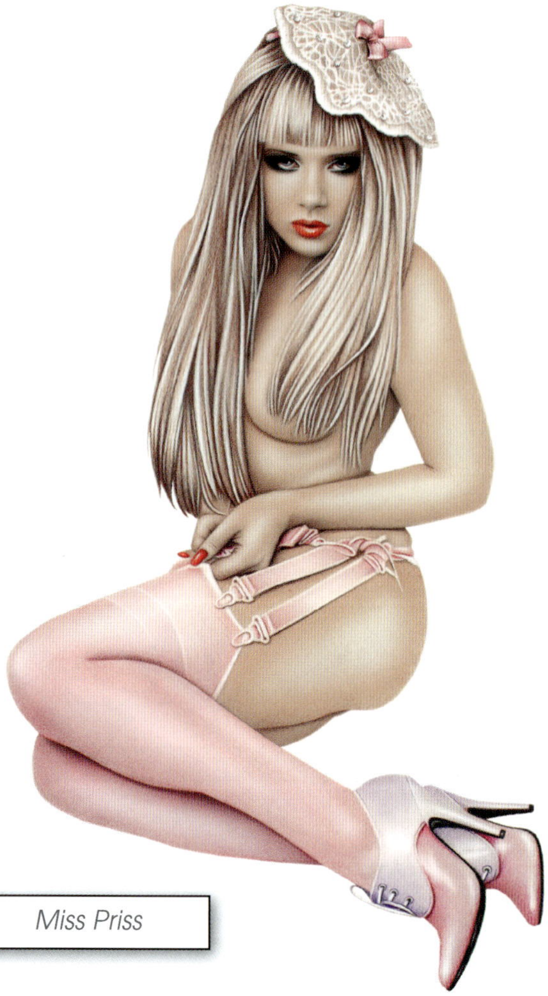

Miss Priss

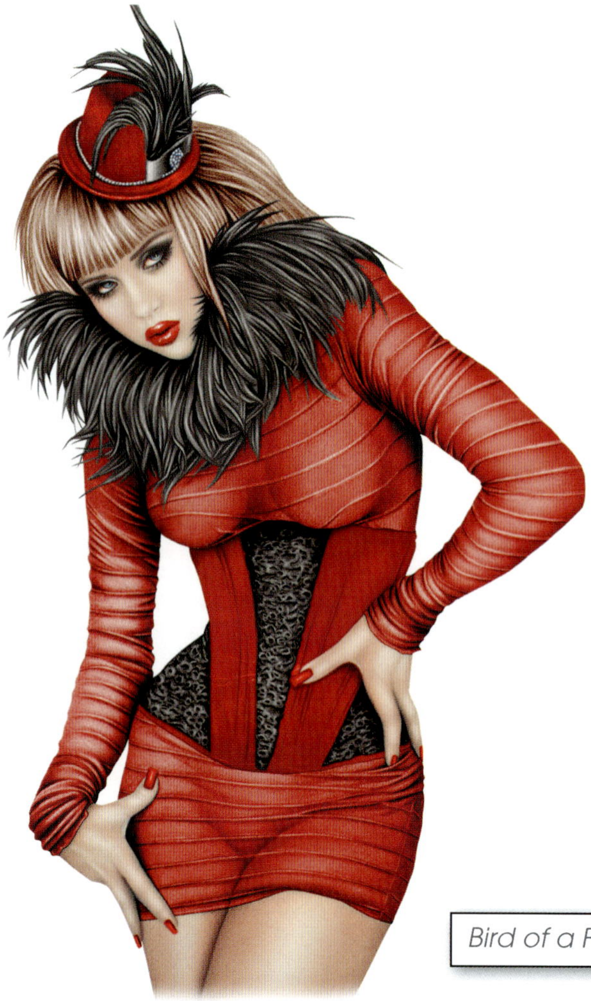

Bird of a Feather

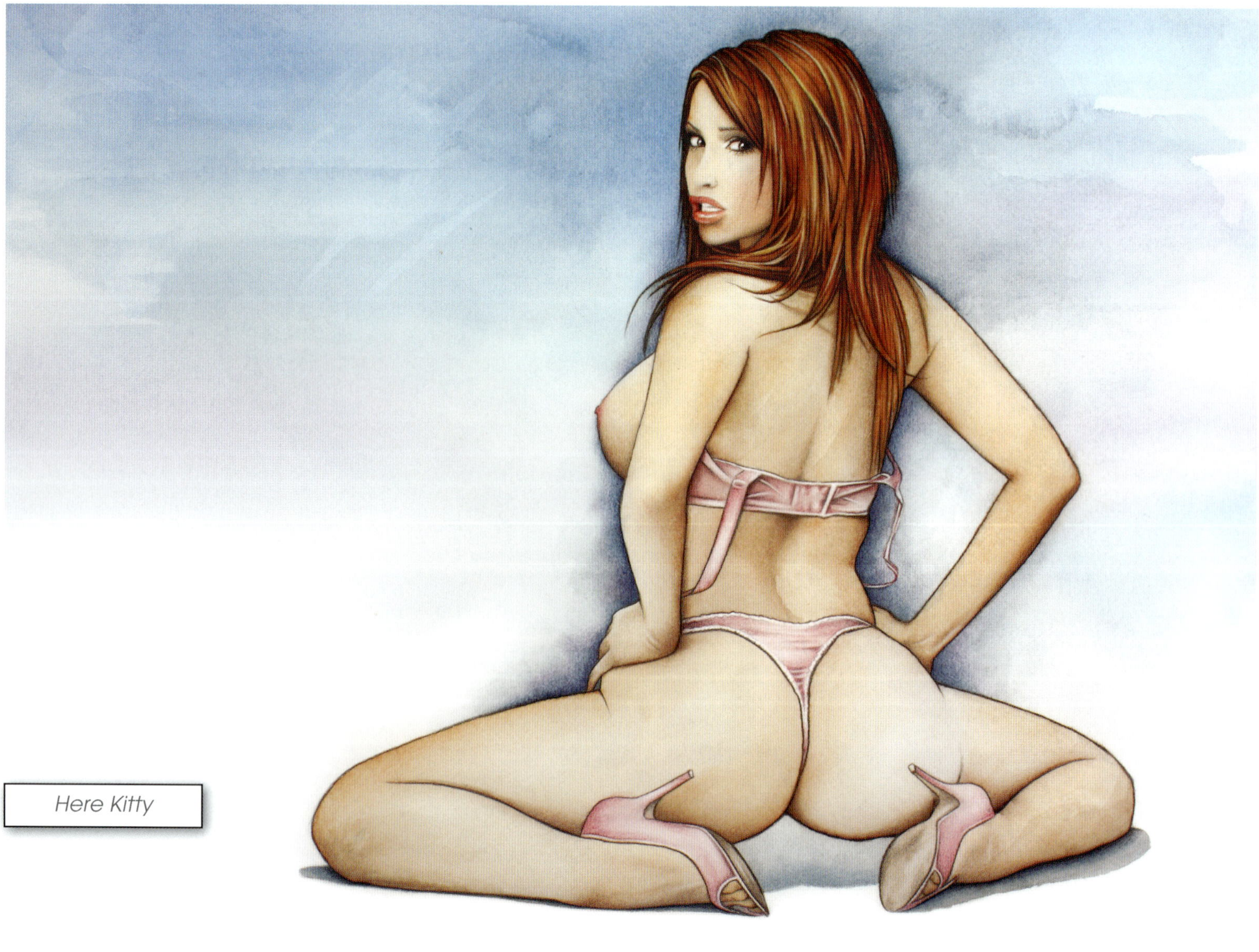

Here Kitty

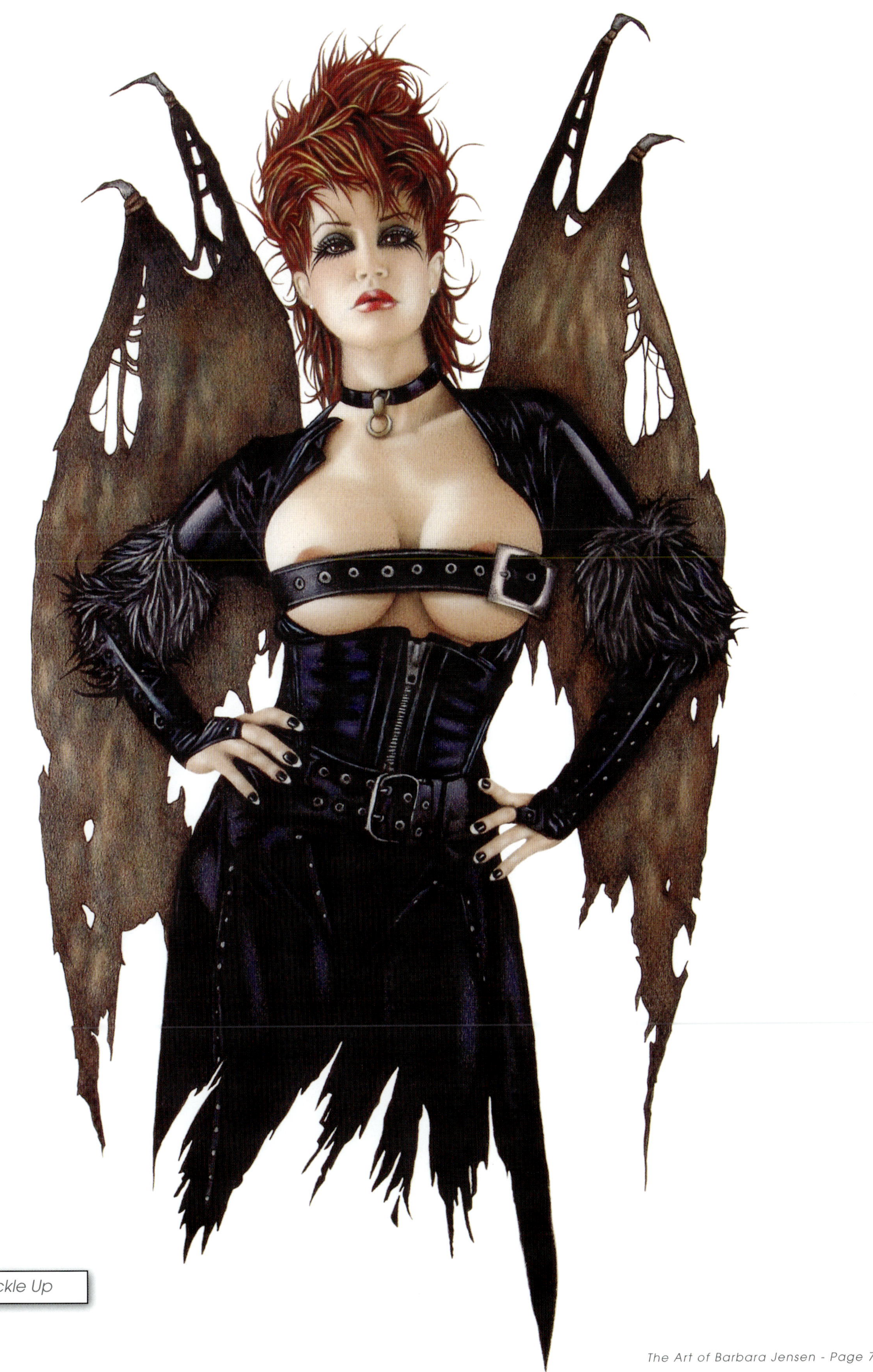

Buckle Up

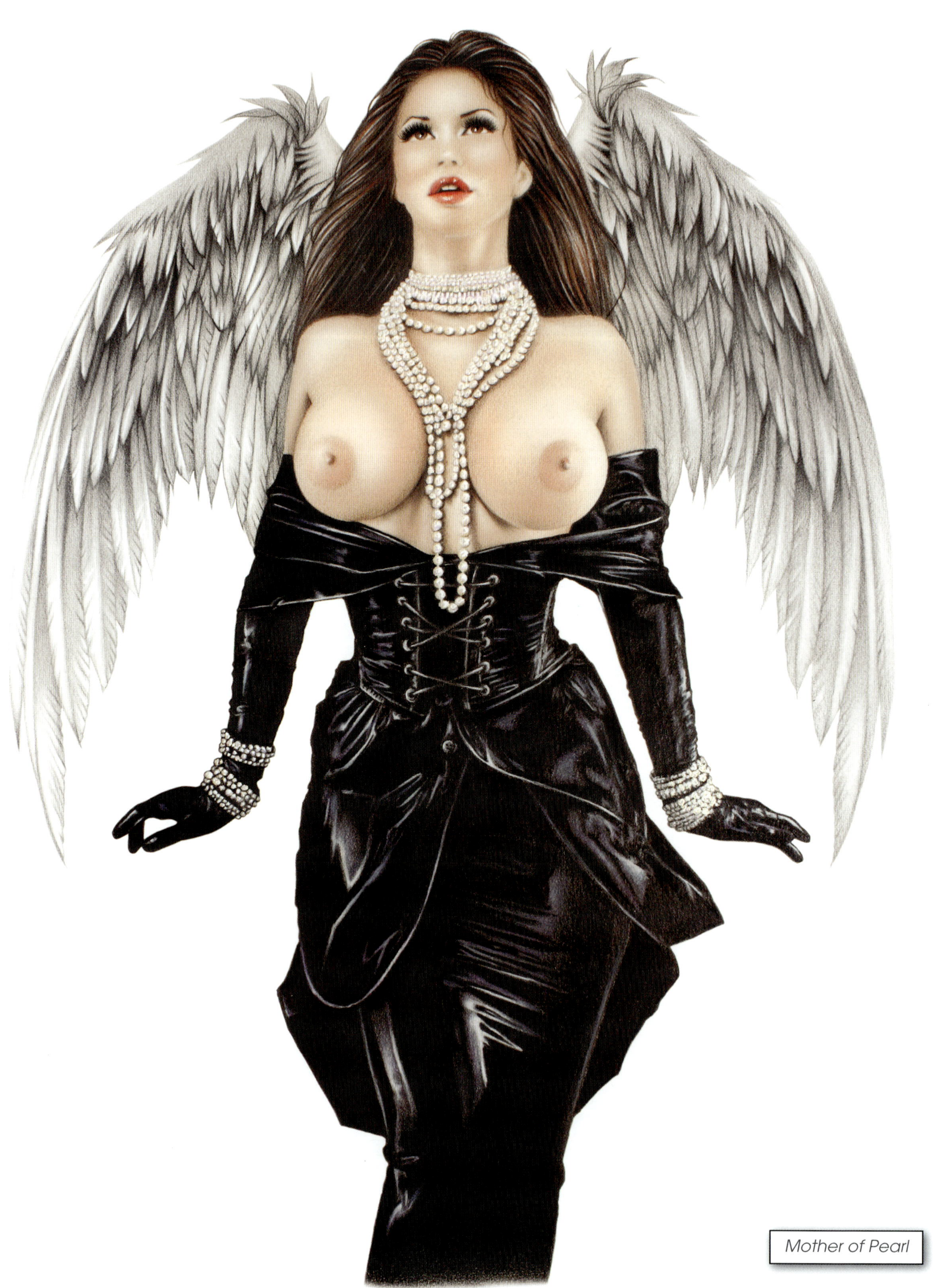

Mother of Pearl

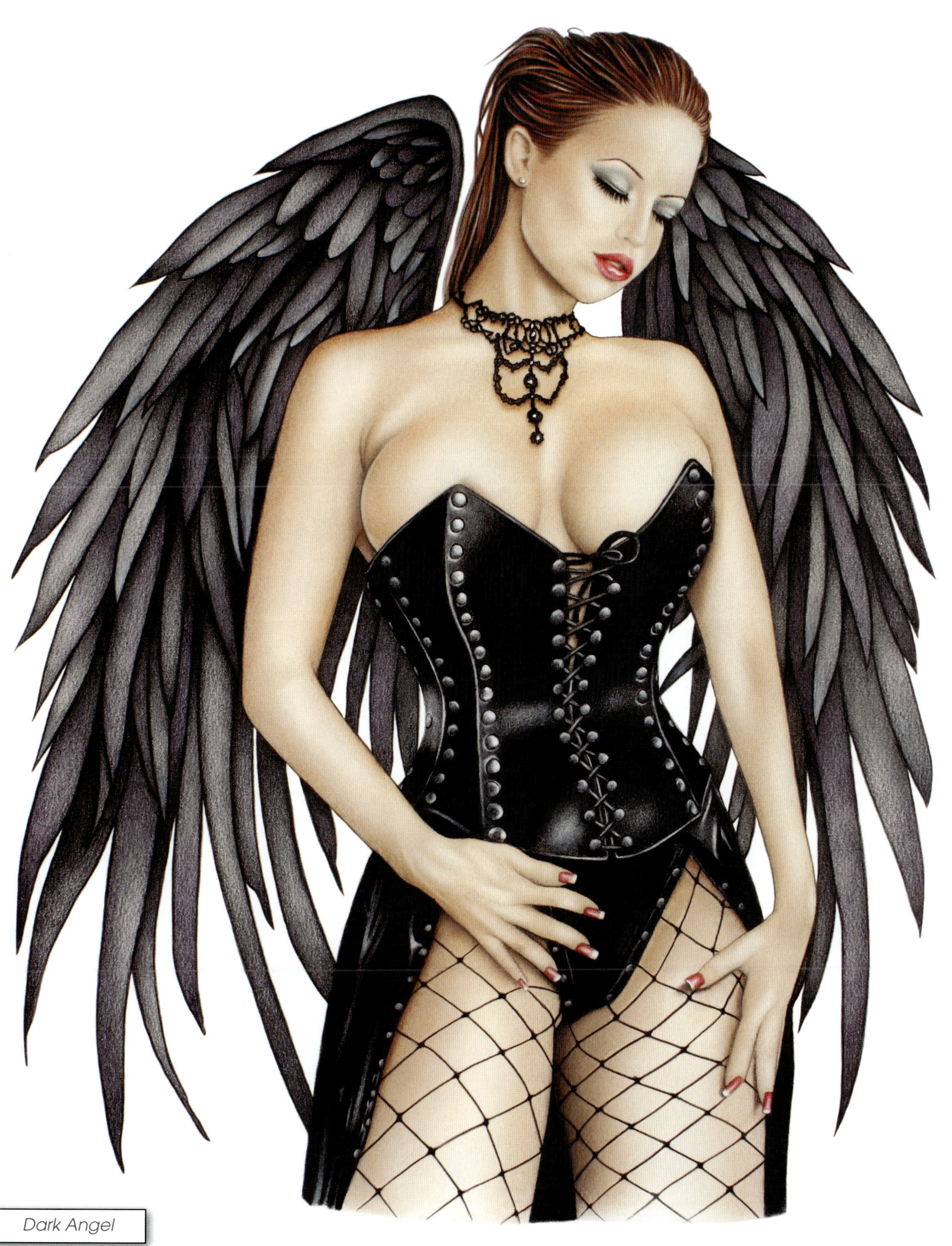

Dark Angel

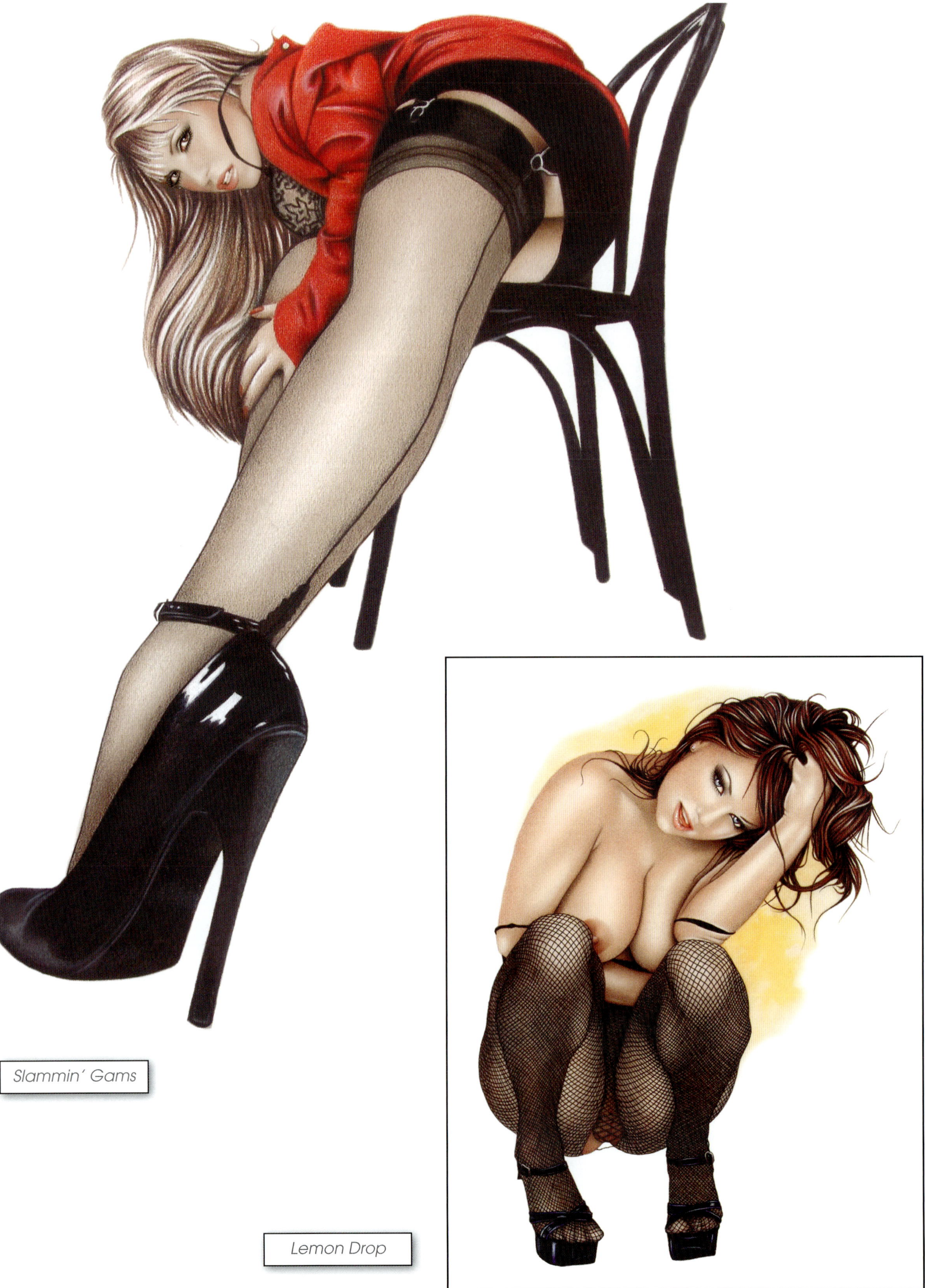

Slammin' Gams

Lemon Drop

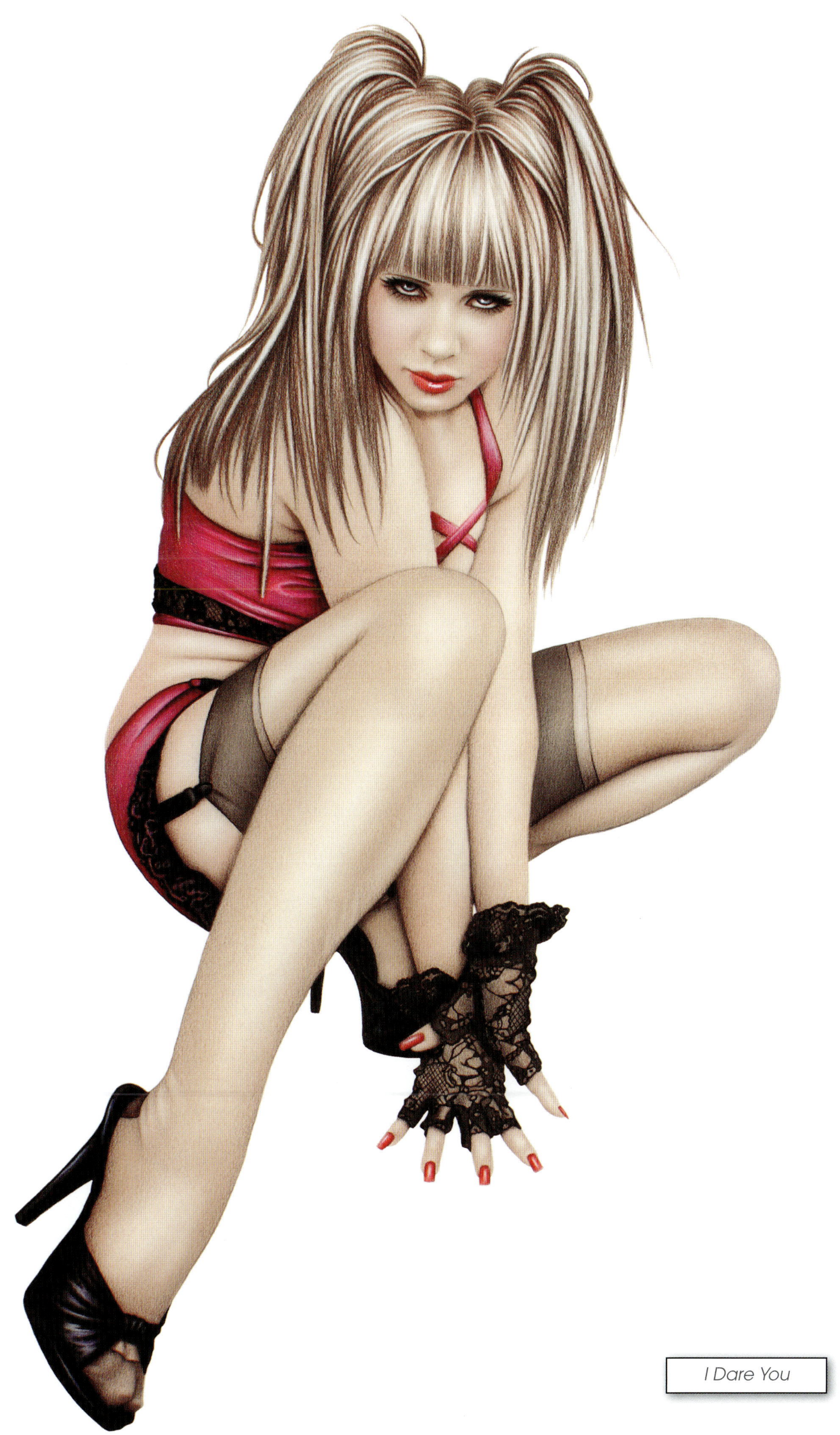

I Dare You

Pure Vintage

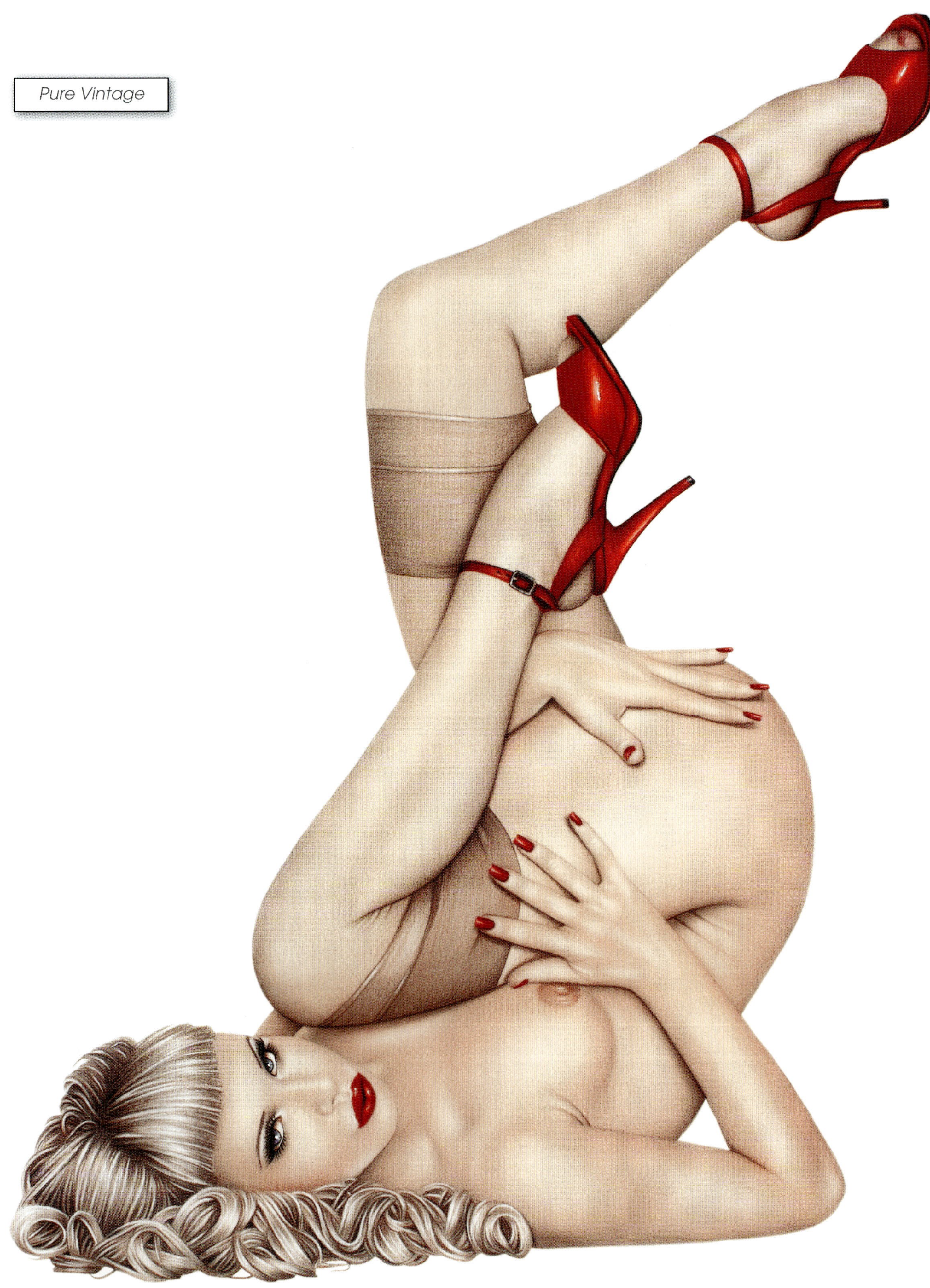

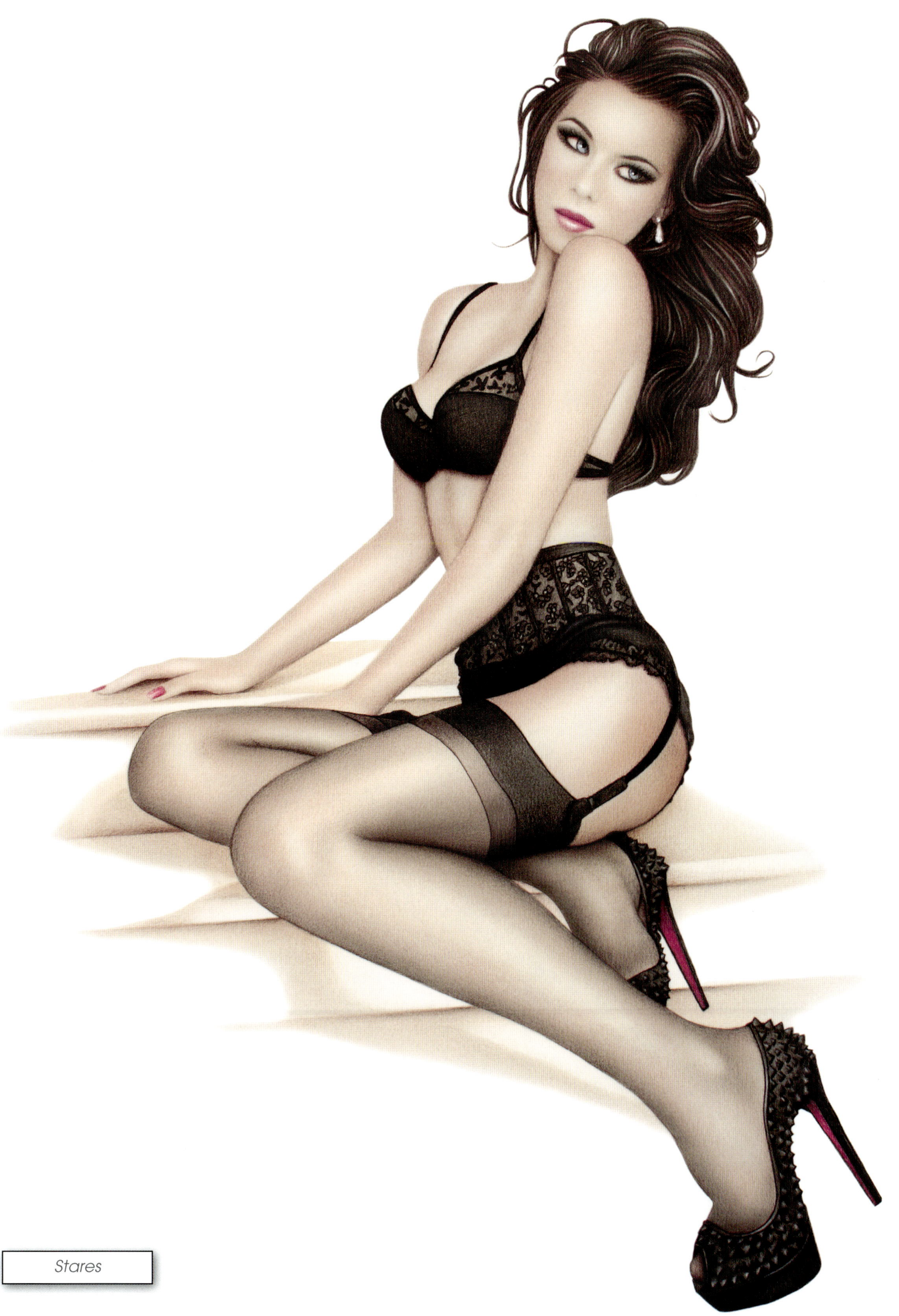

Stares

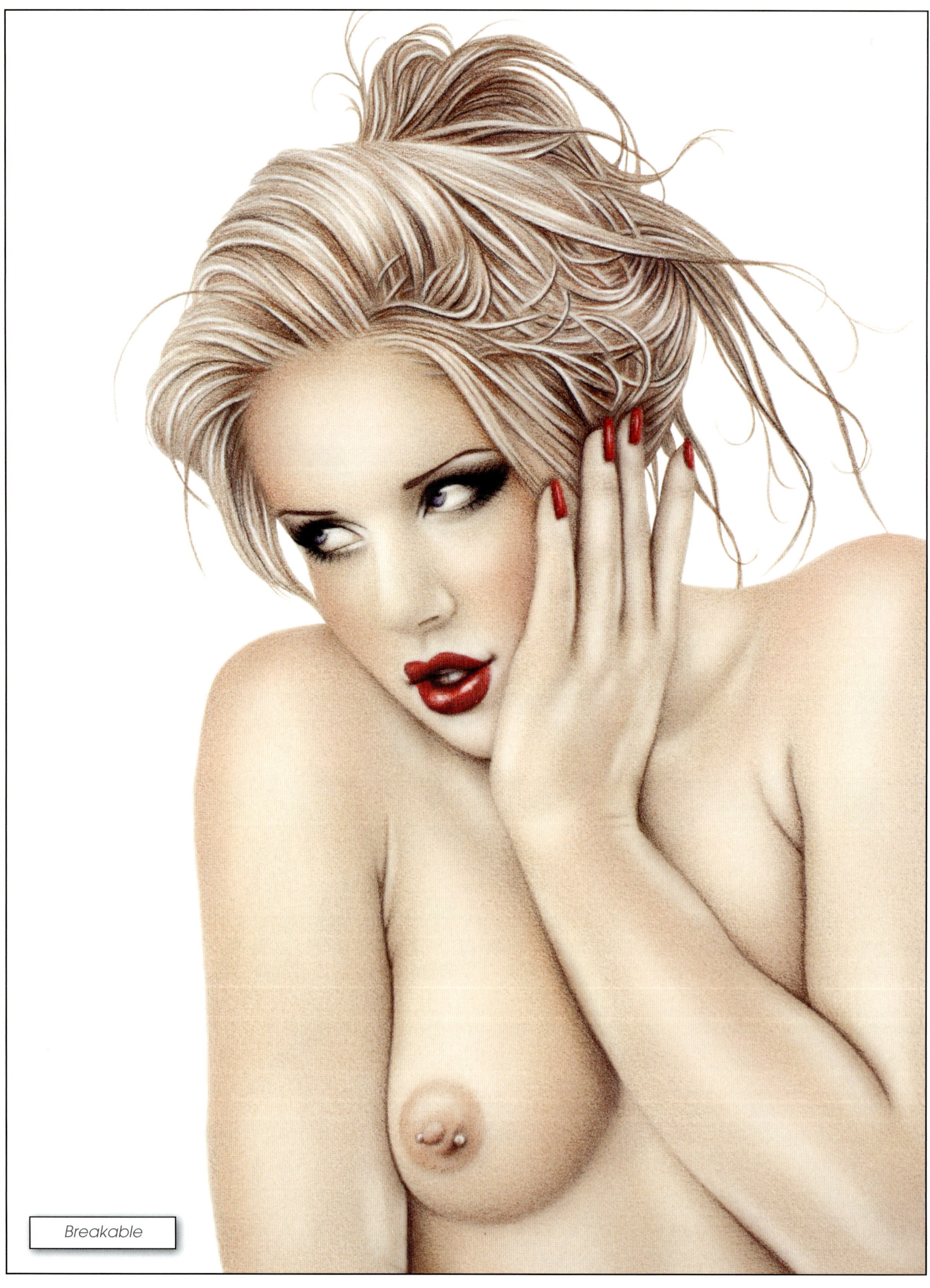

Breakable

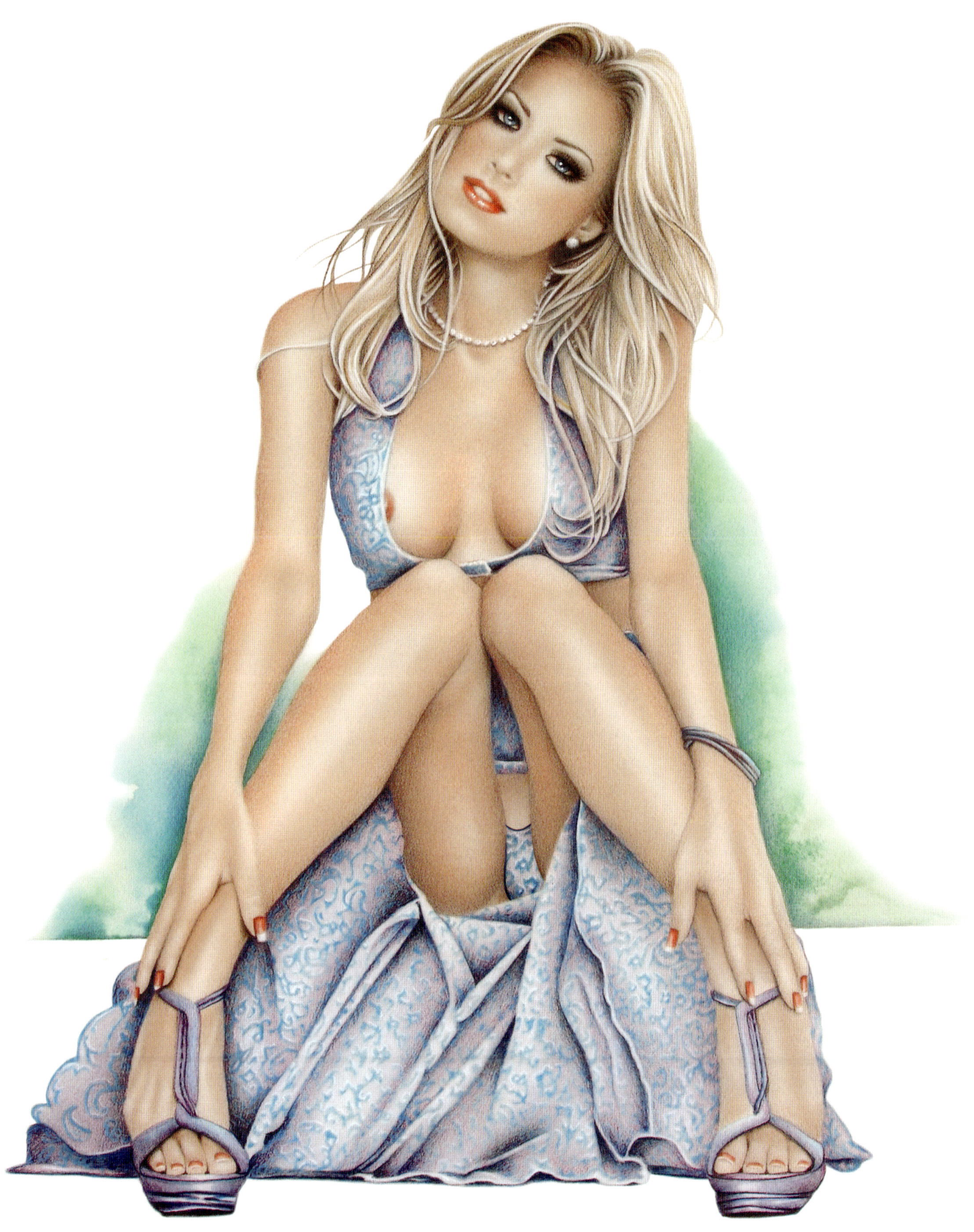

Peek-a-Blue

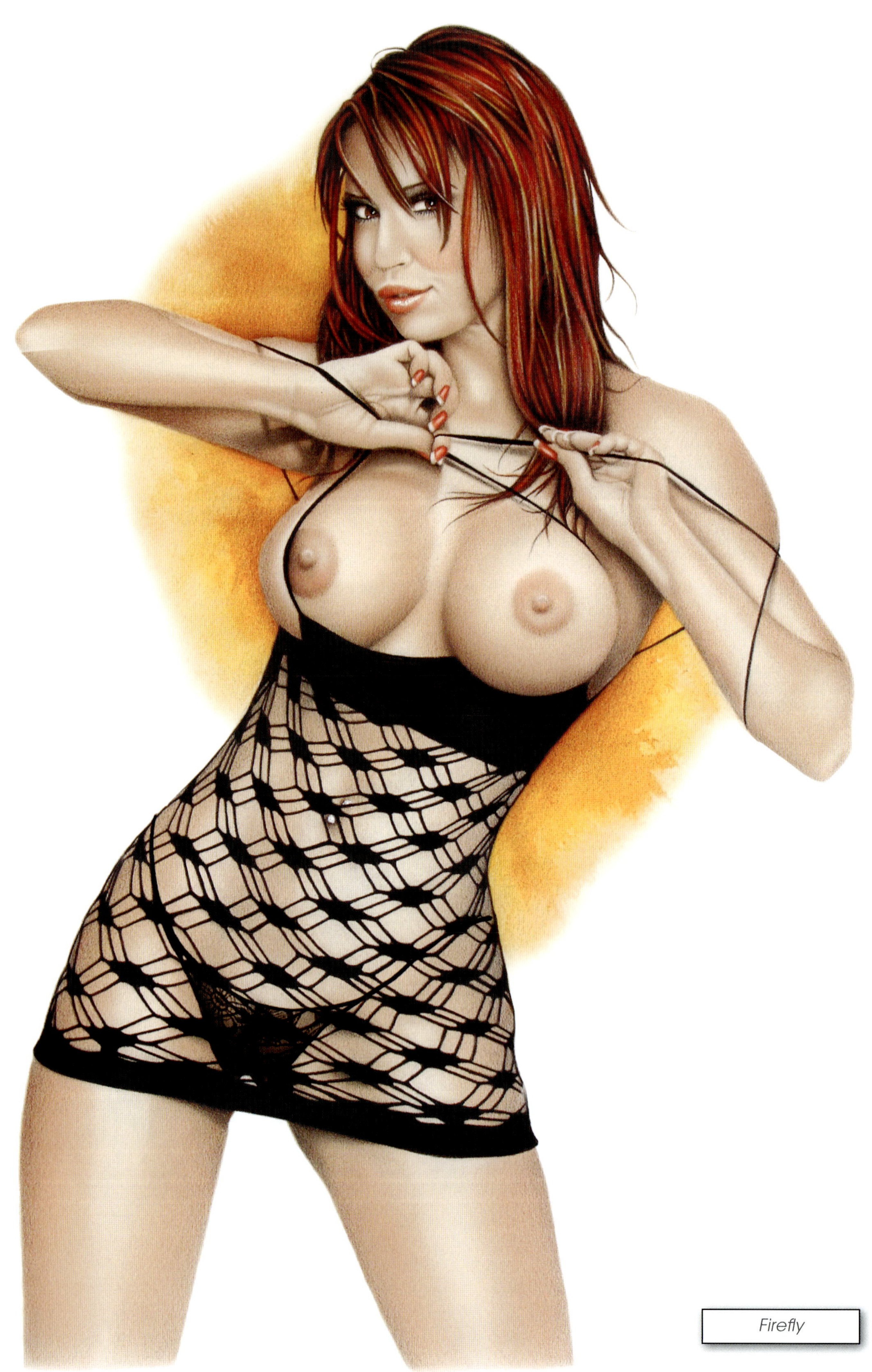

Firefly

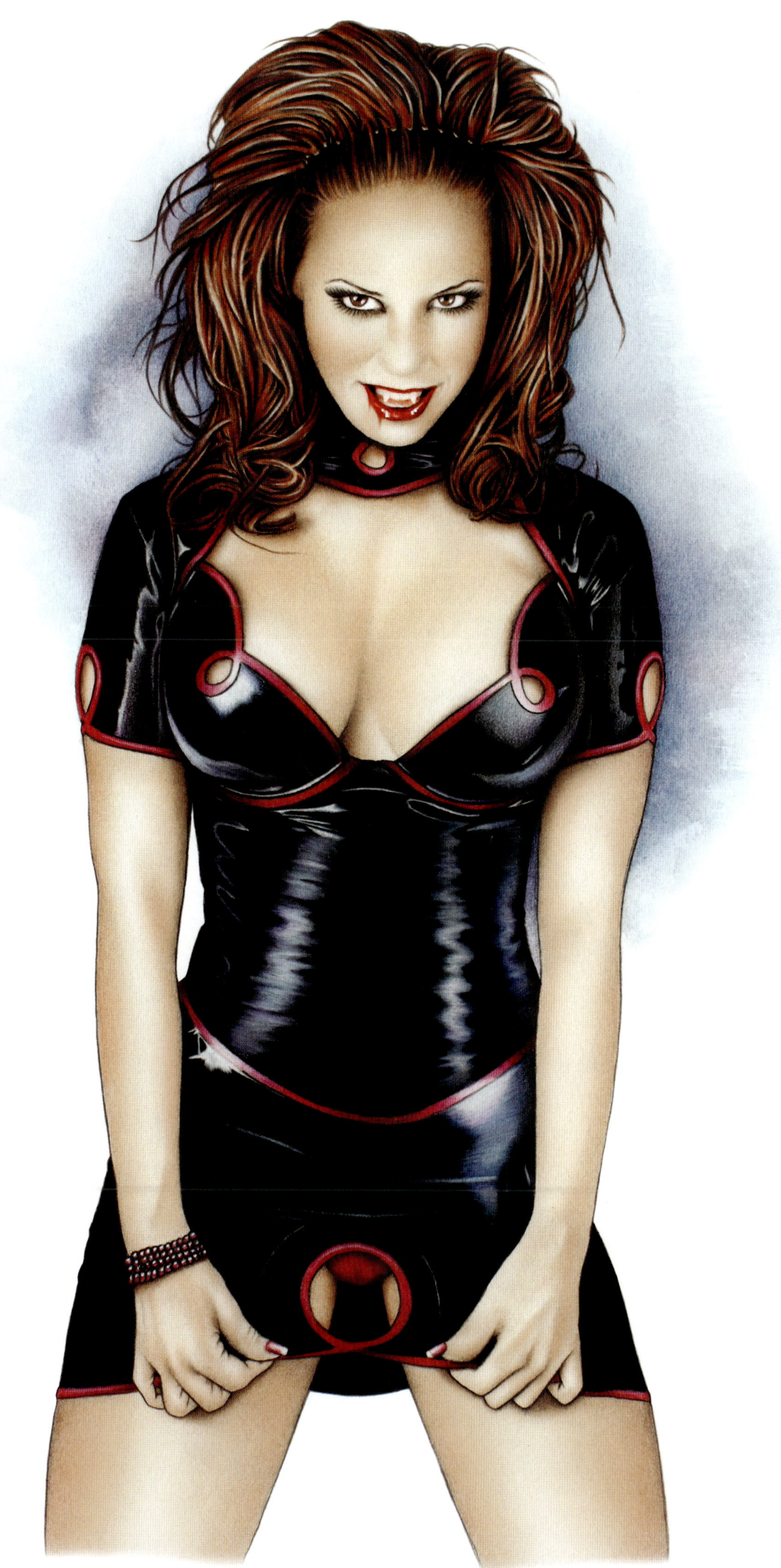

Secret Places

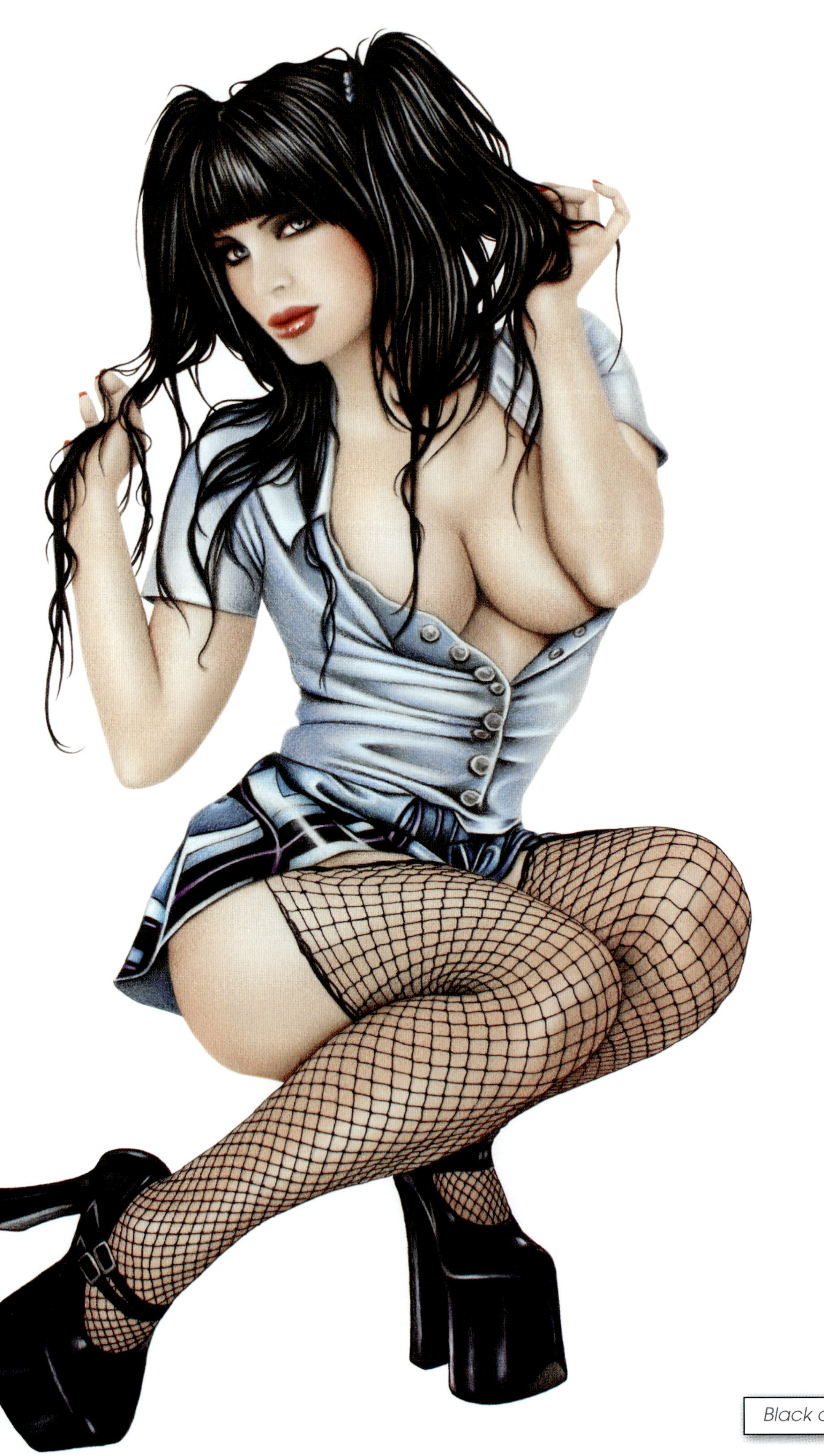

Black and Blue

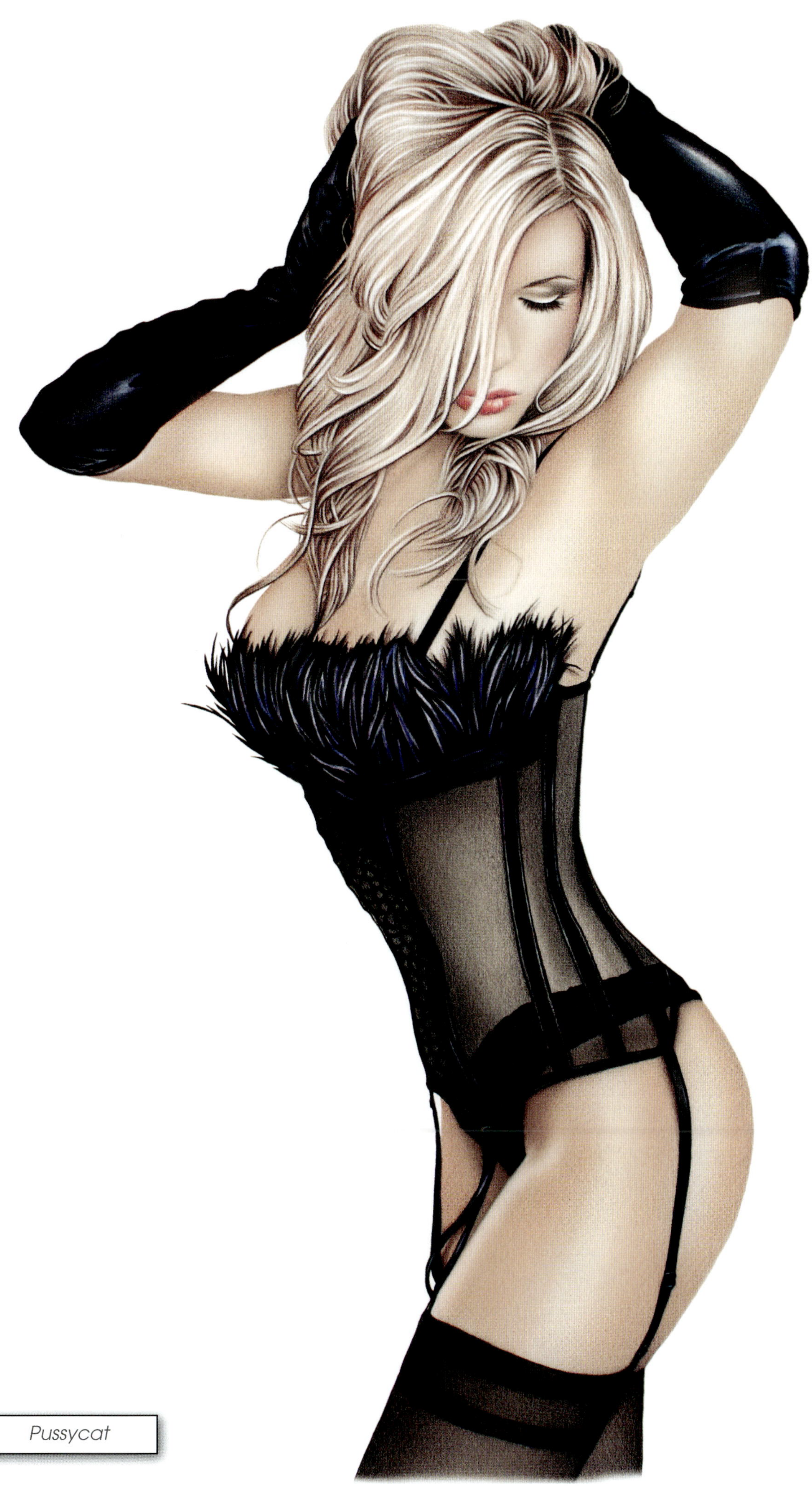

Pussycat

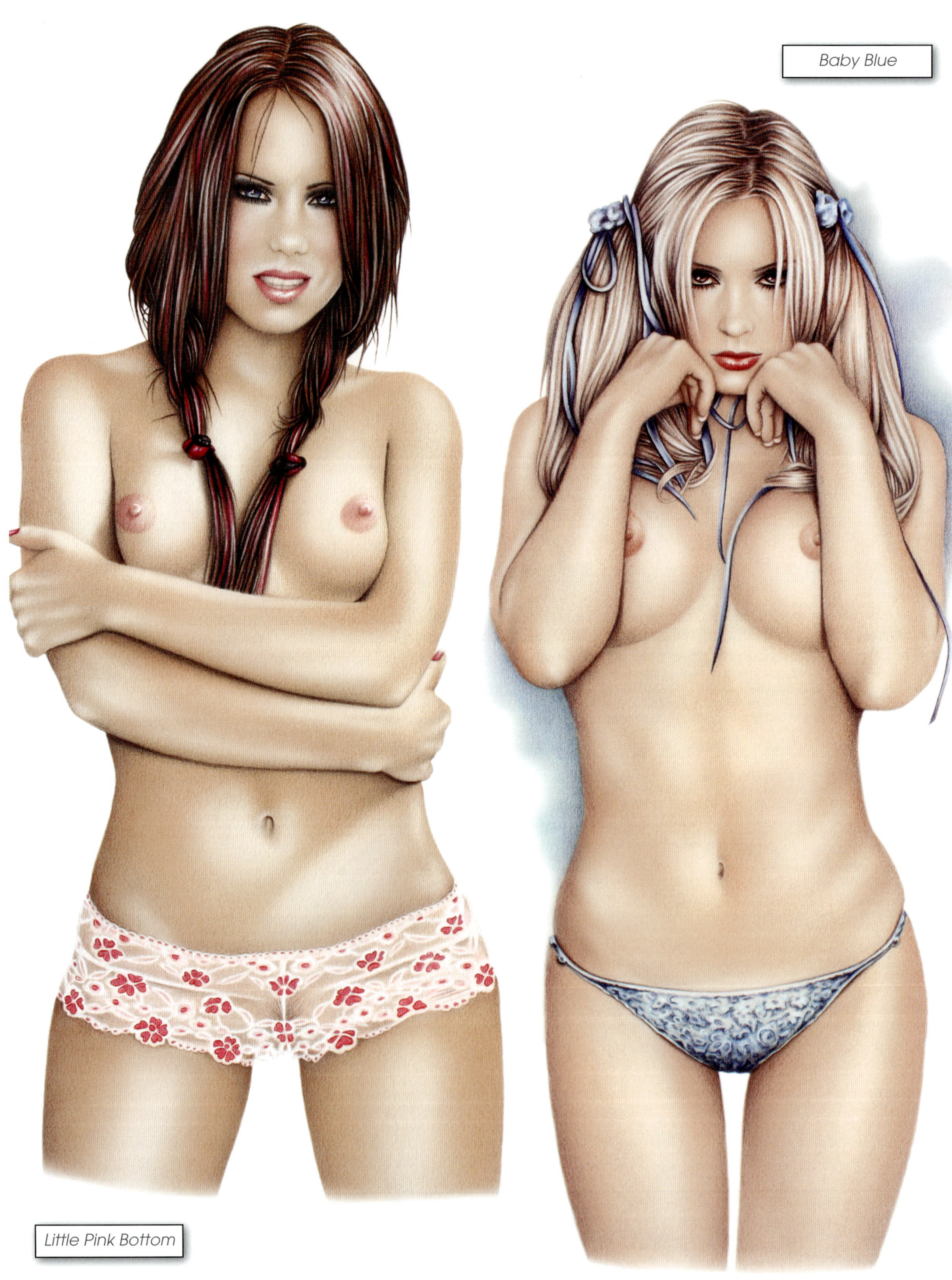
Baby Blue
Little Pink Bottom

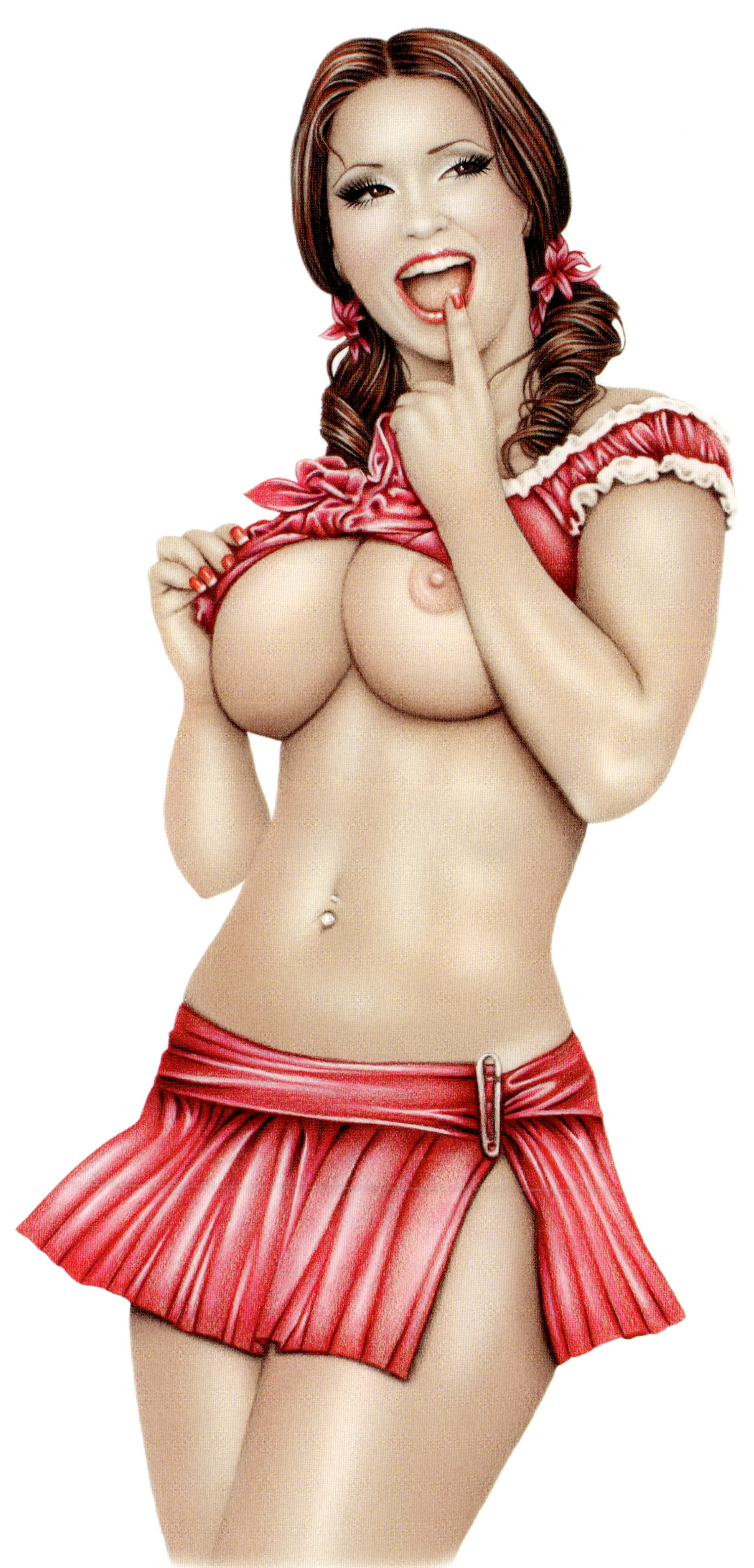

Bedazzled

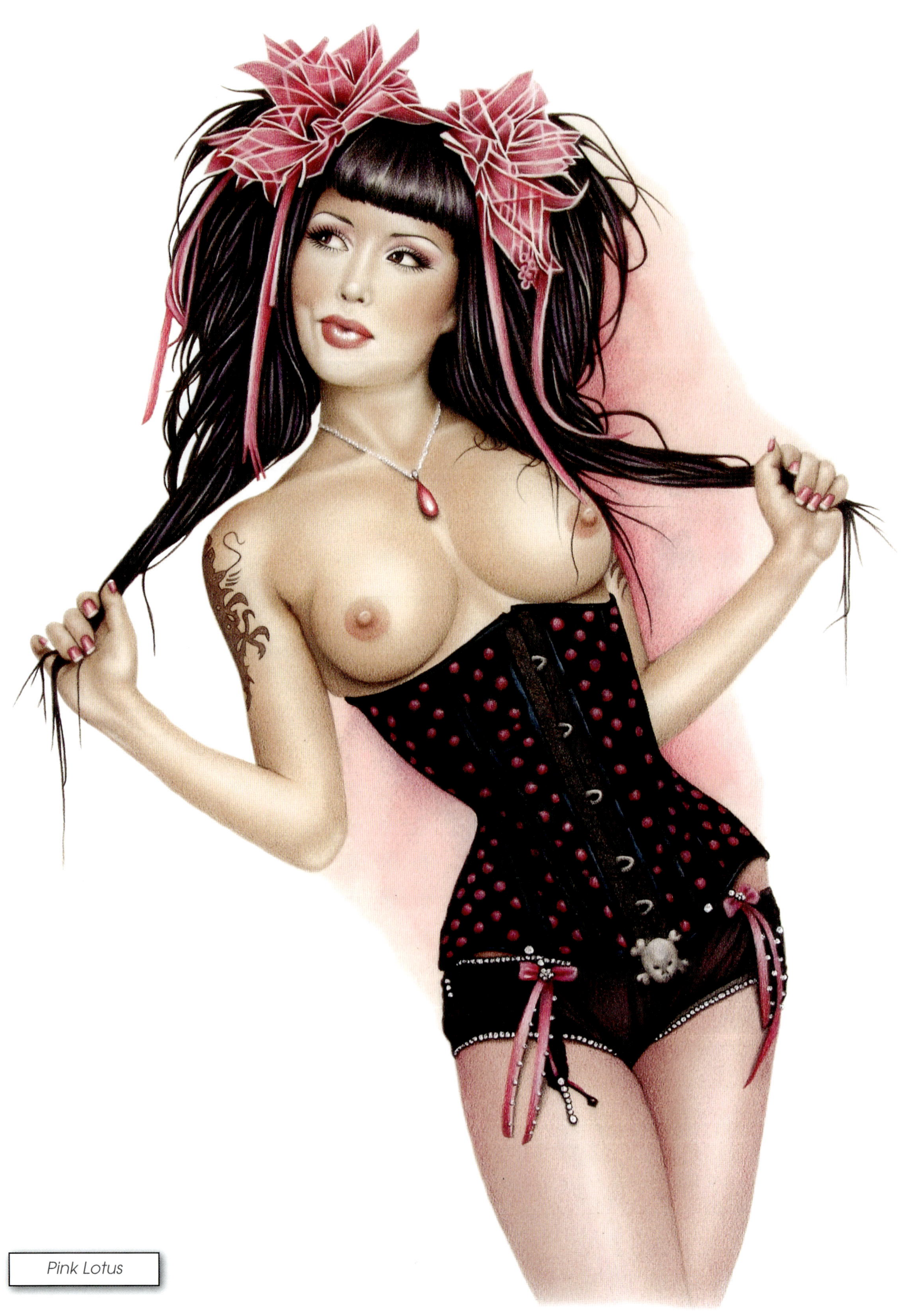

Pink Lotus

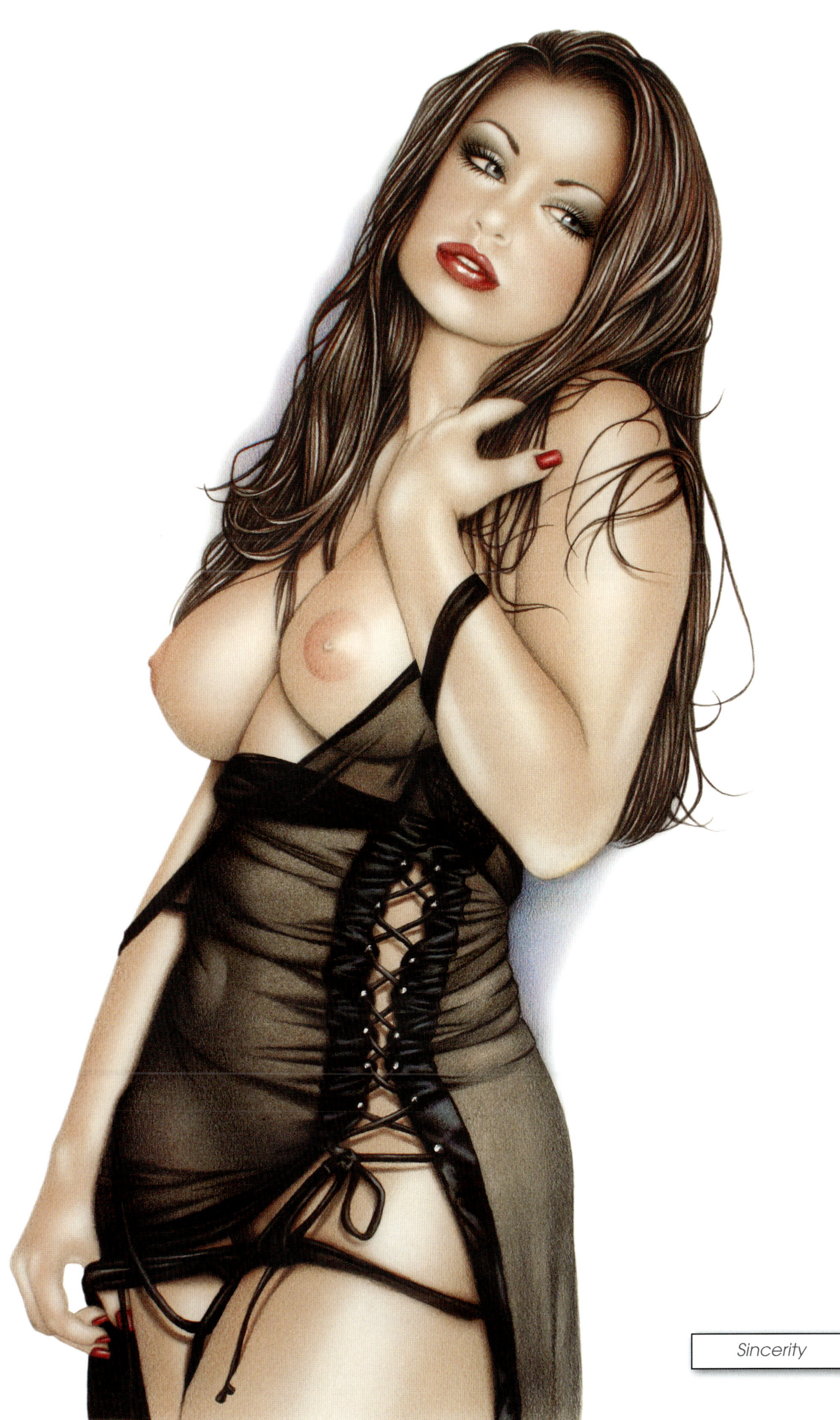

Sincerity

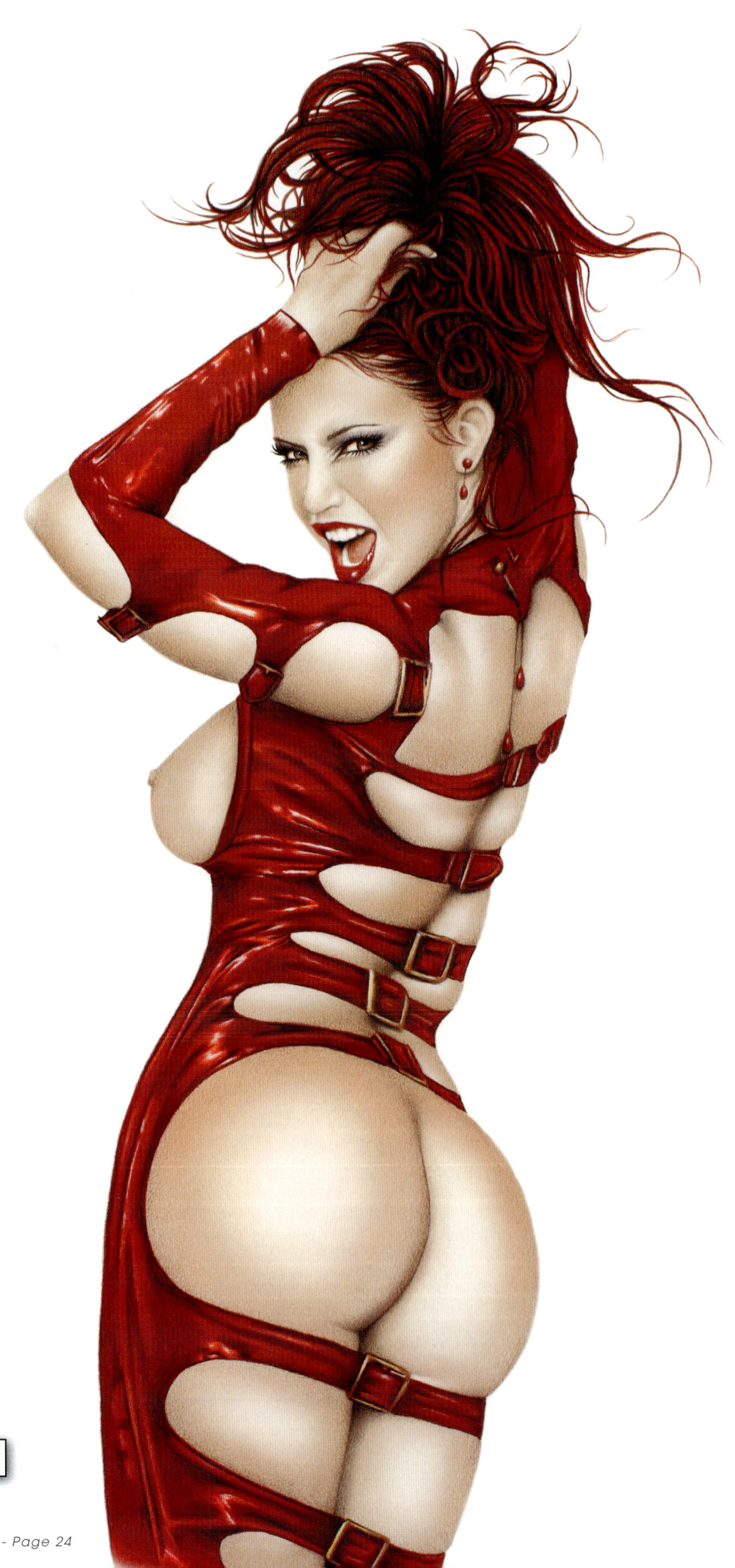

Femme Aflame

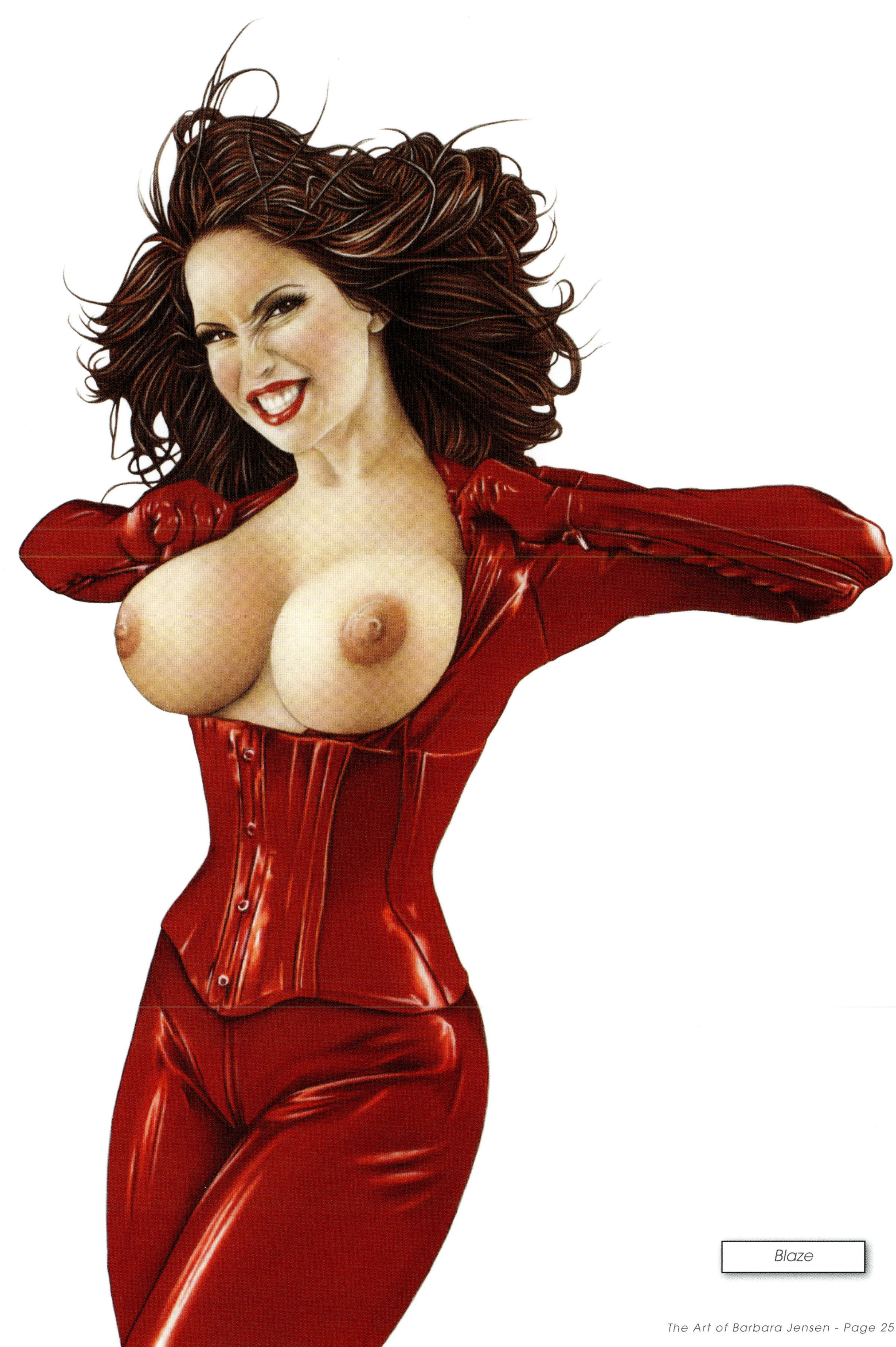

Blaze

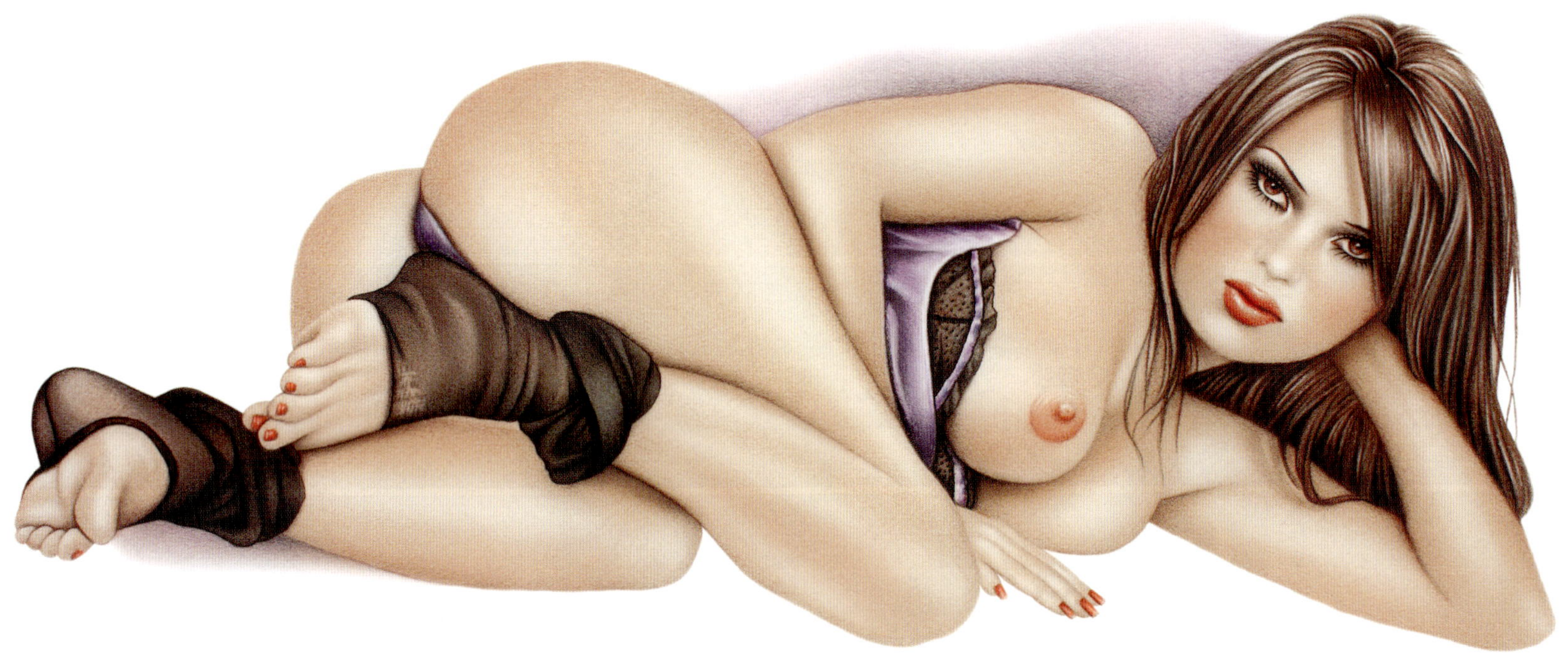

Stocking Stuffer

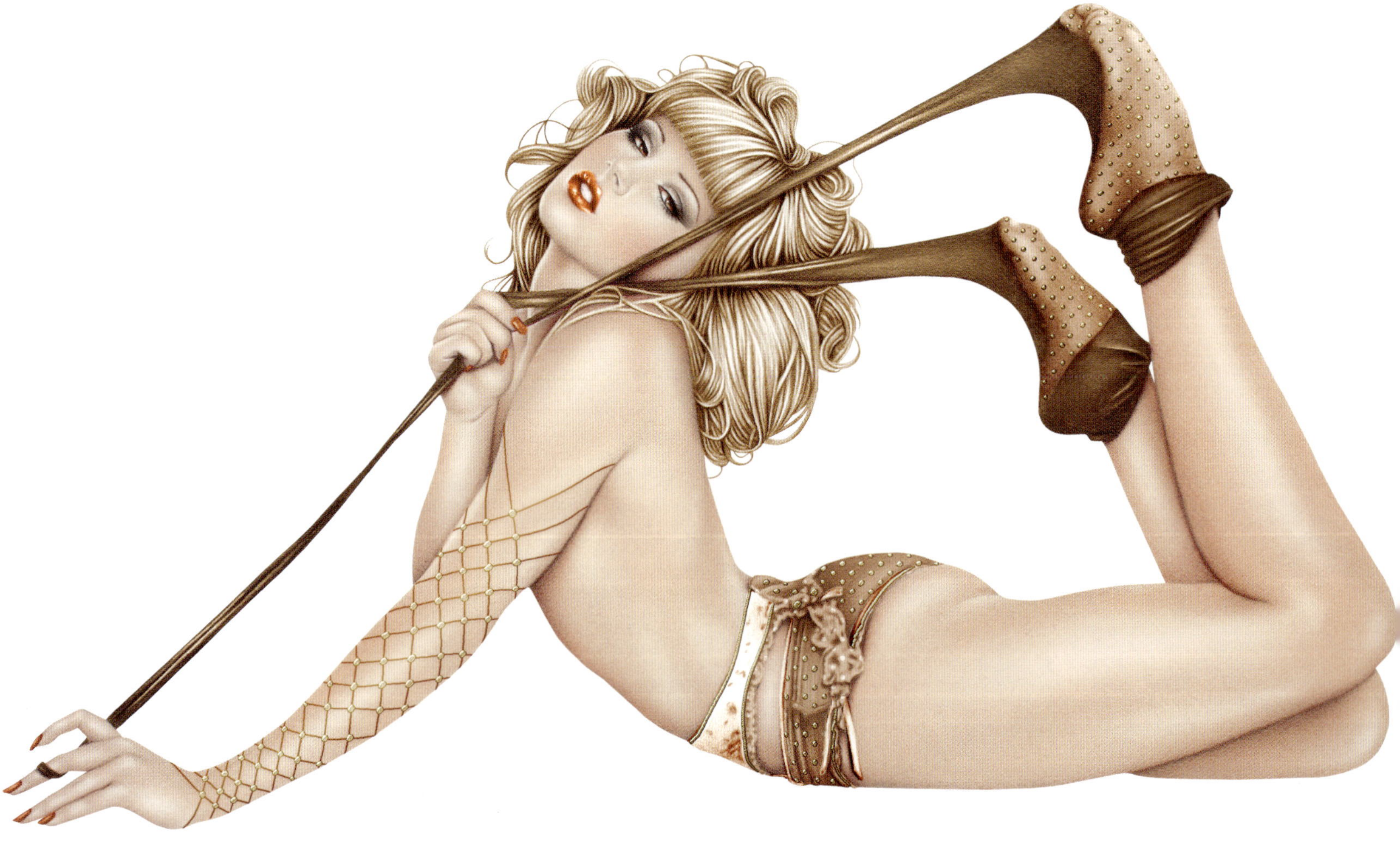

Hose Play

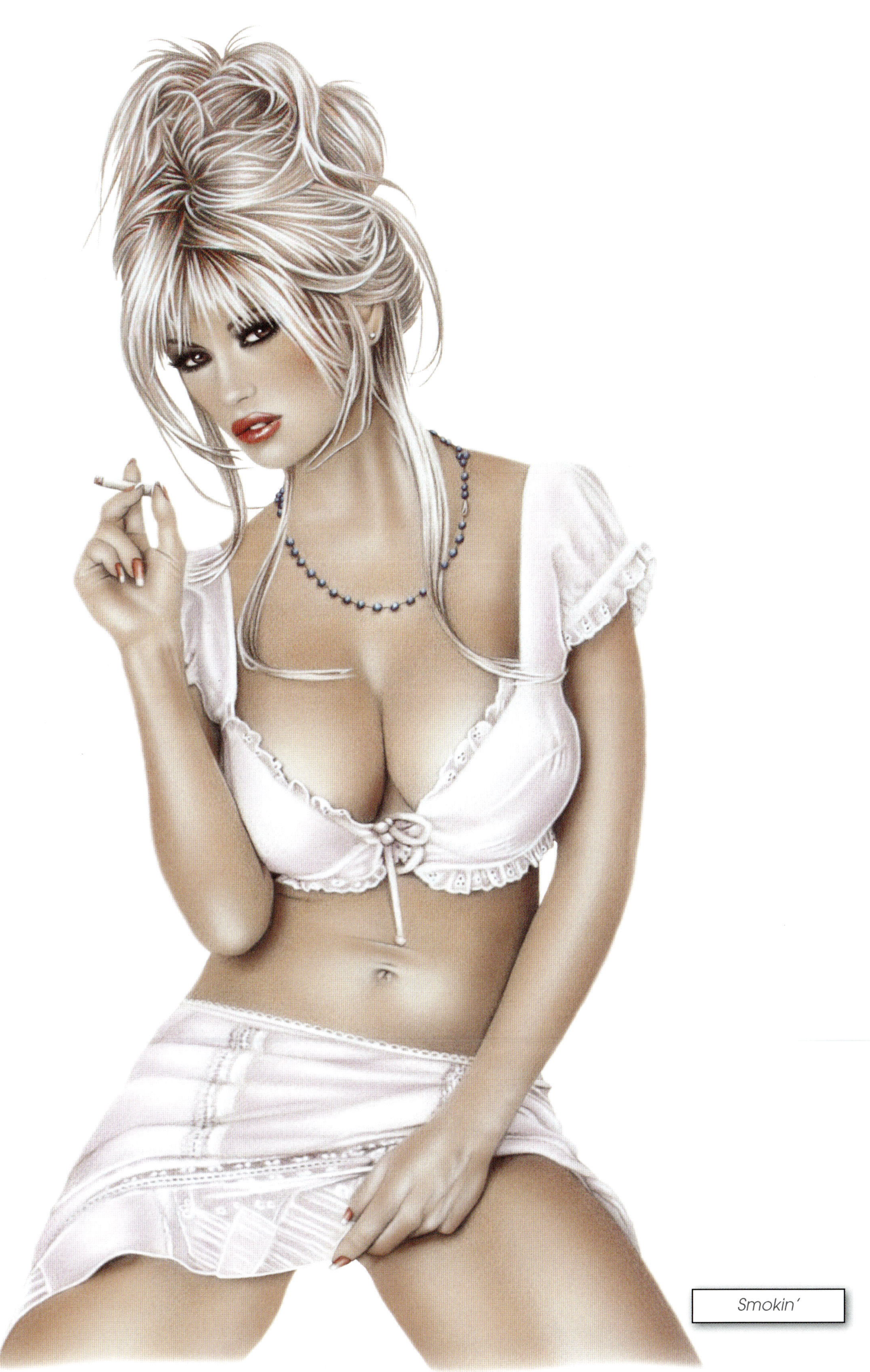

Smokin'

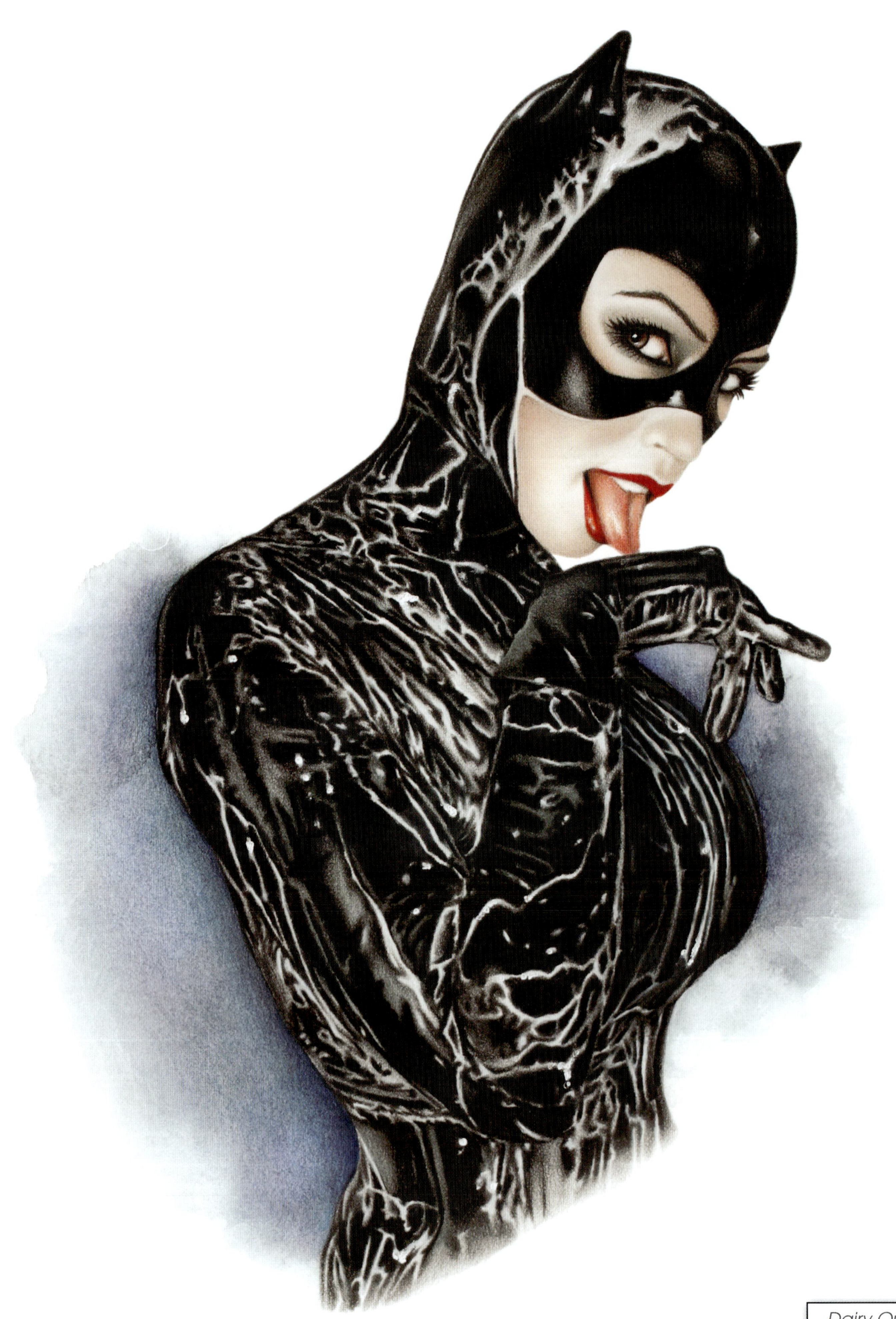

Dairy Queen 1

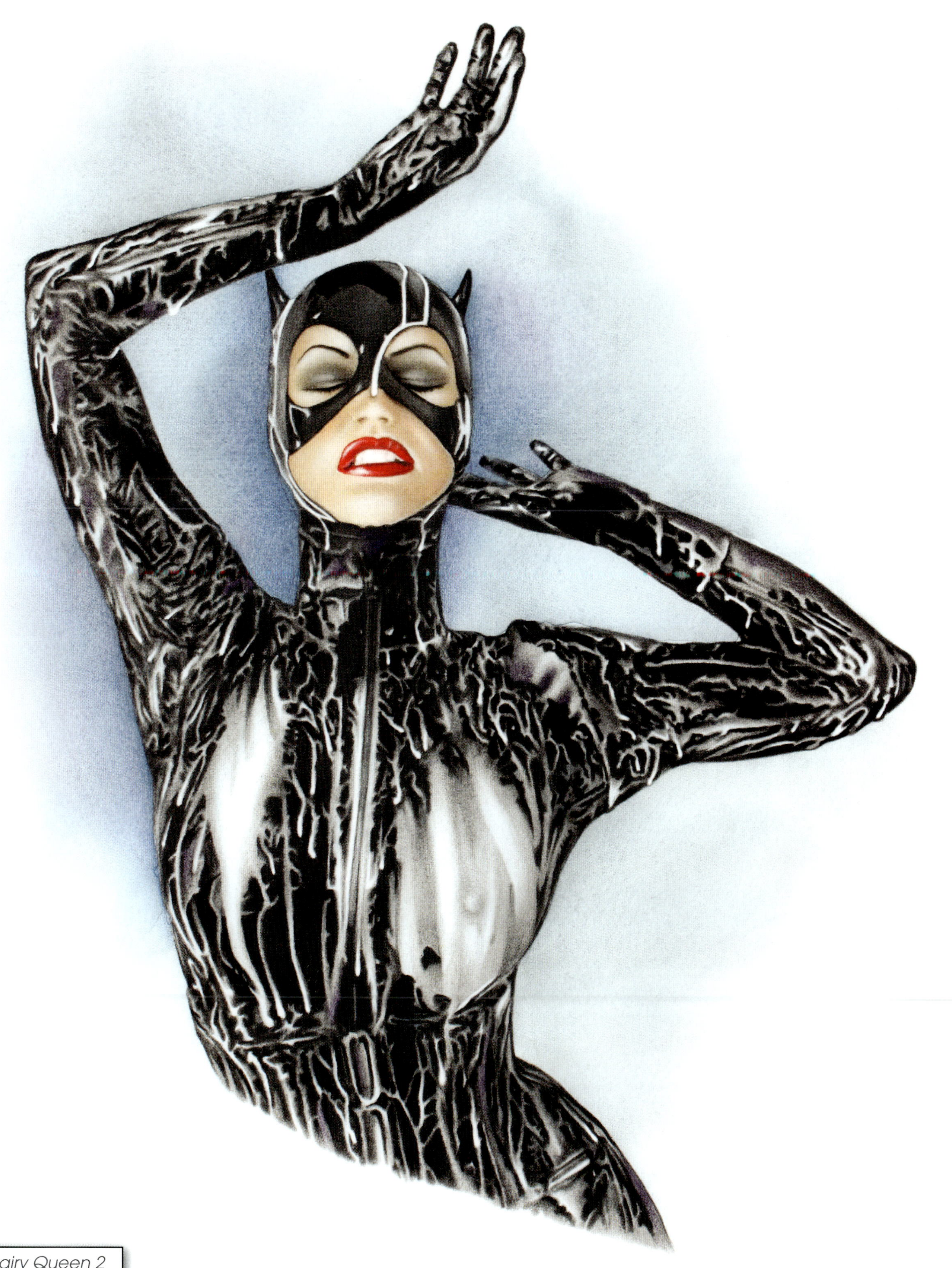

Dairy Queen 2

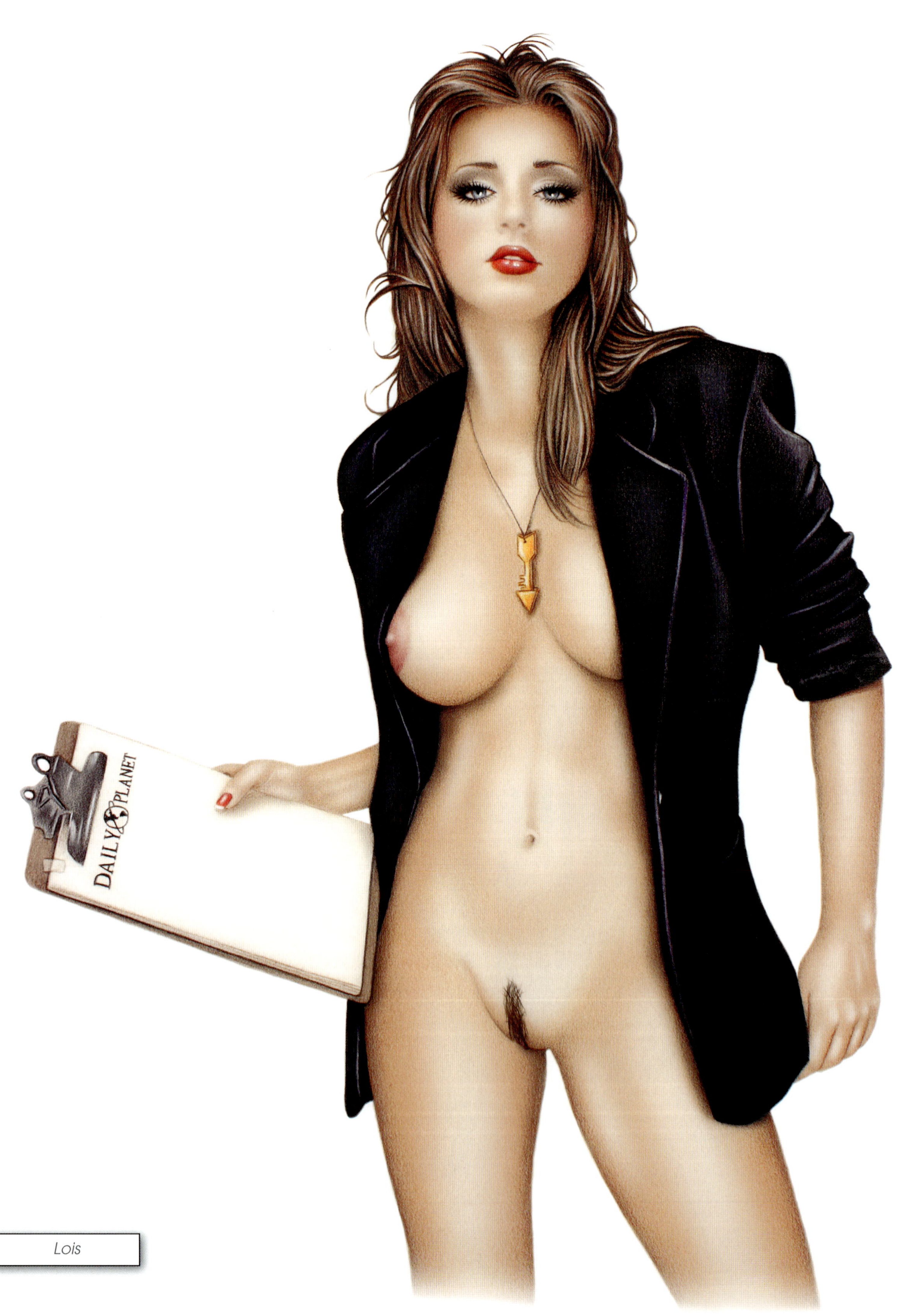

Lois

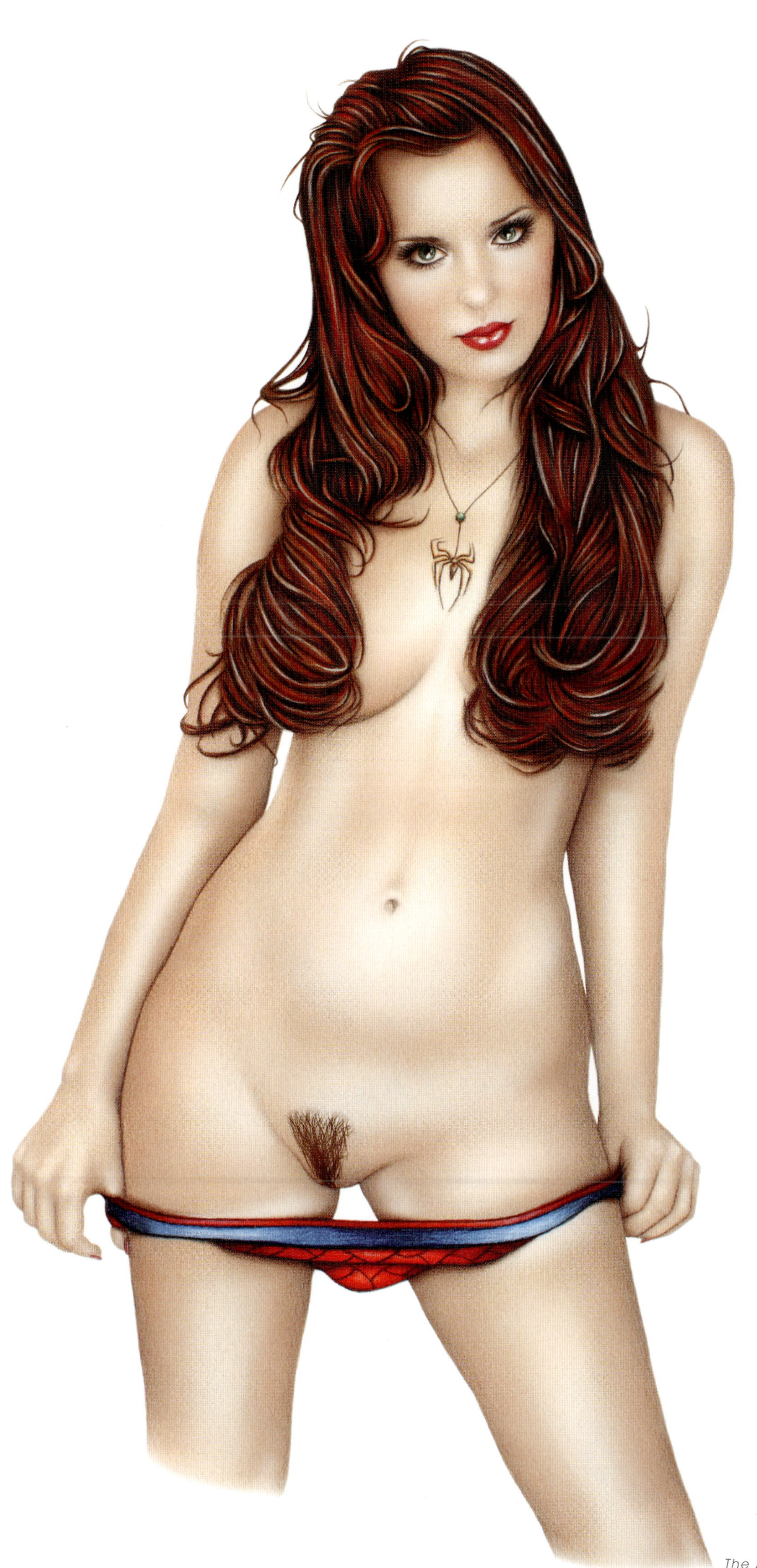

MJ

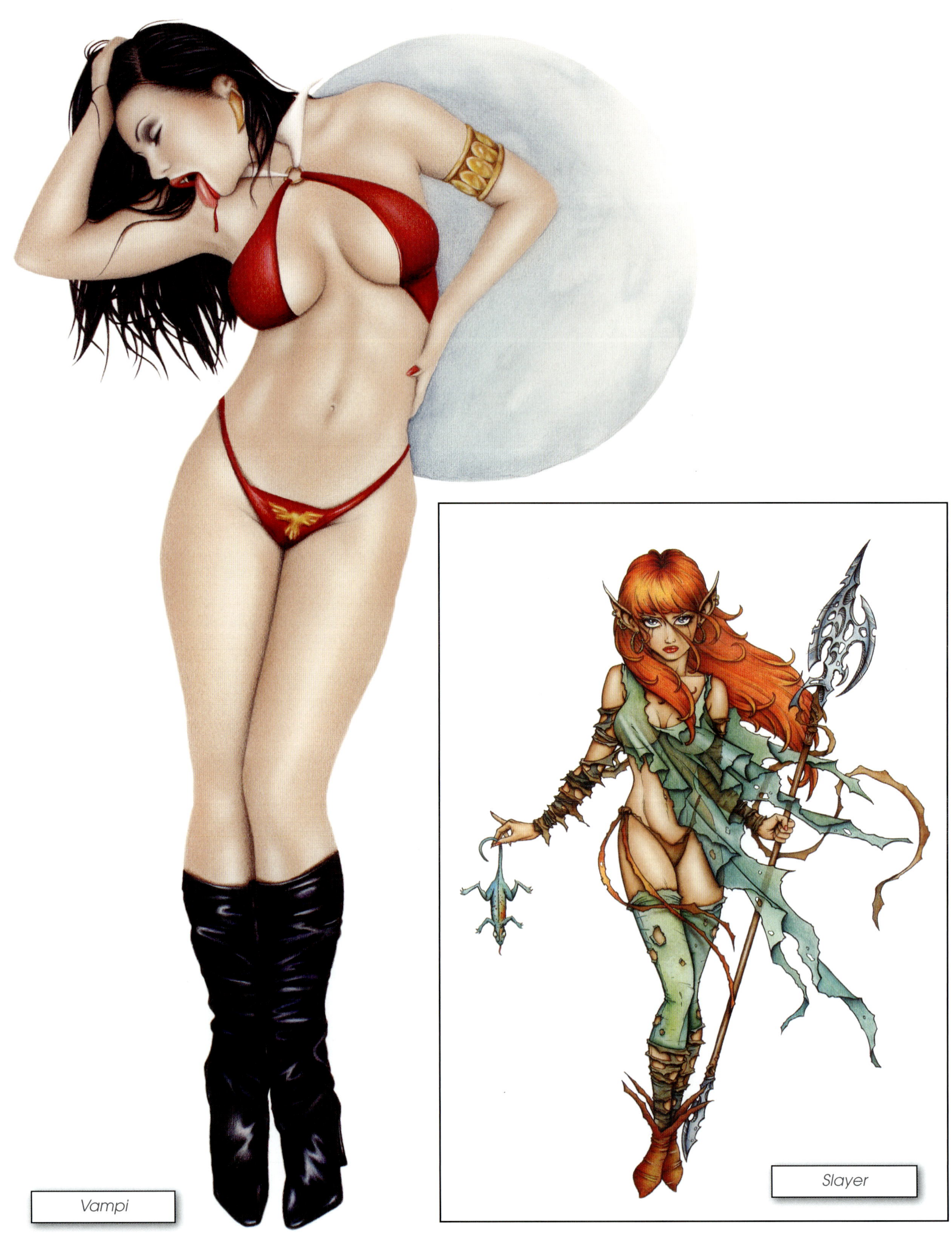

Vampi

Slayer

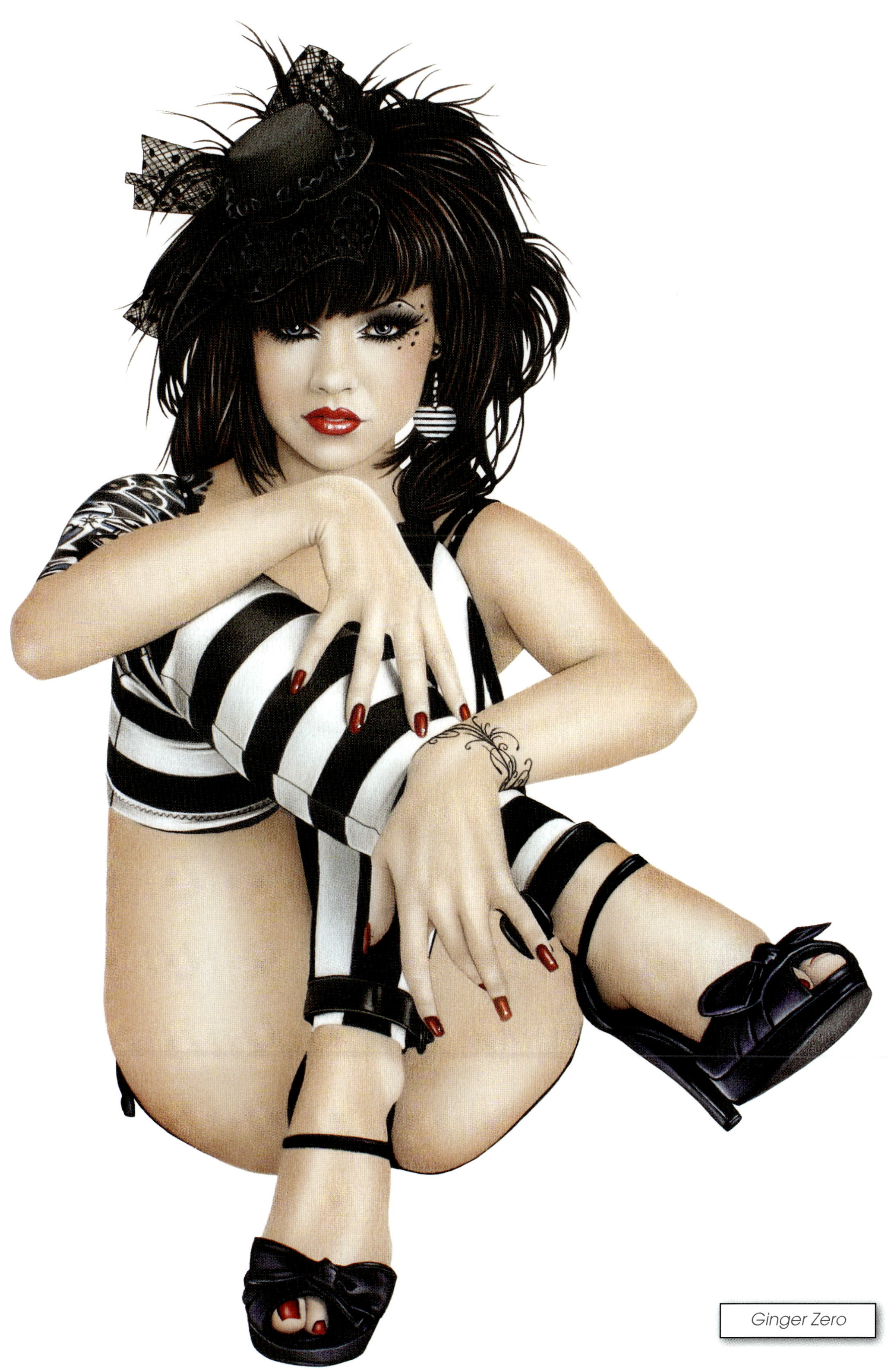

Ginger Zero

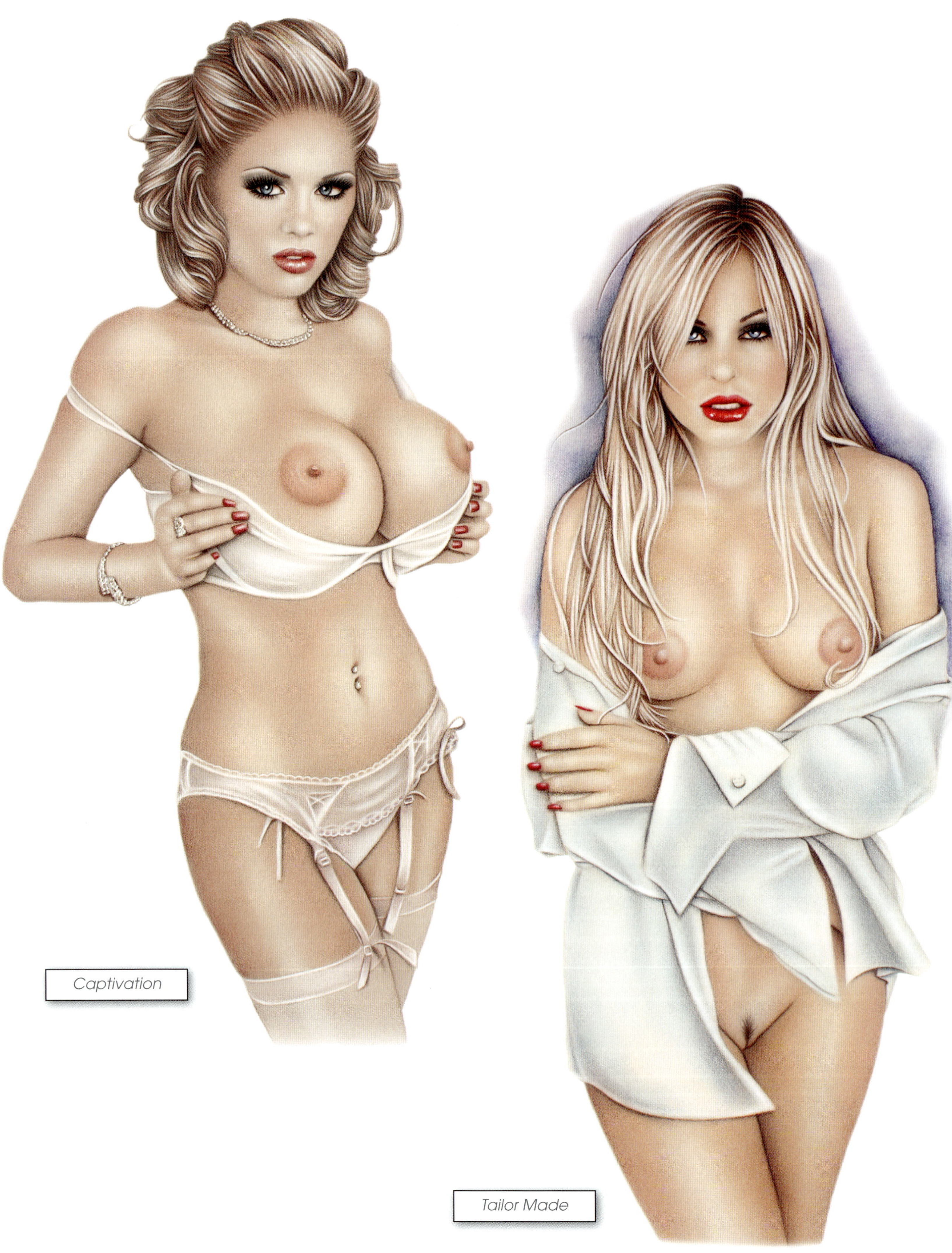

Captivation

Tailor Made

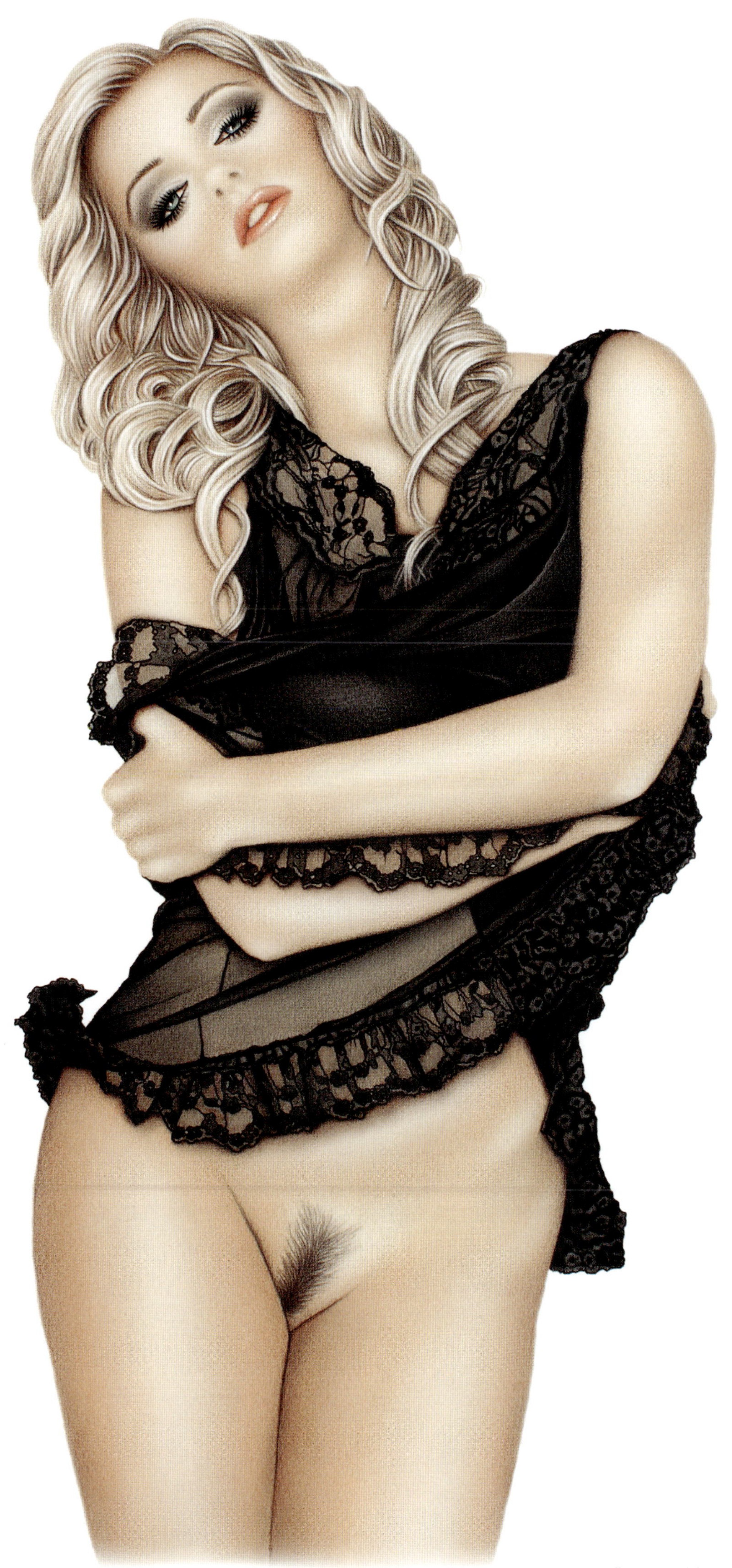

Southern Exposure

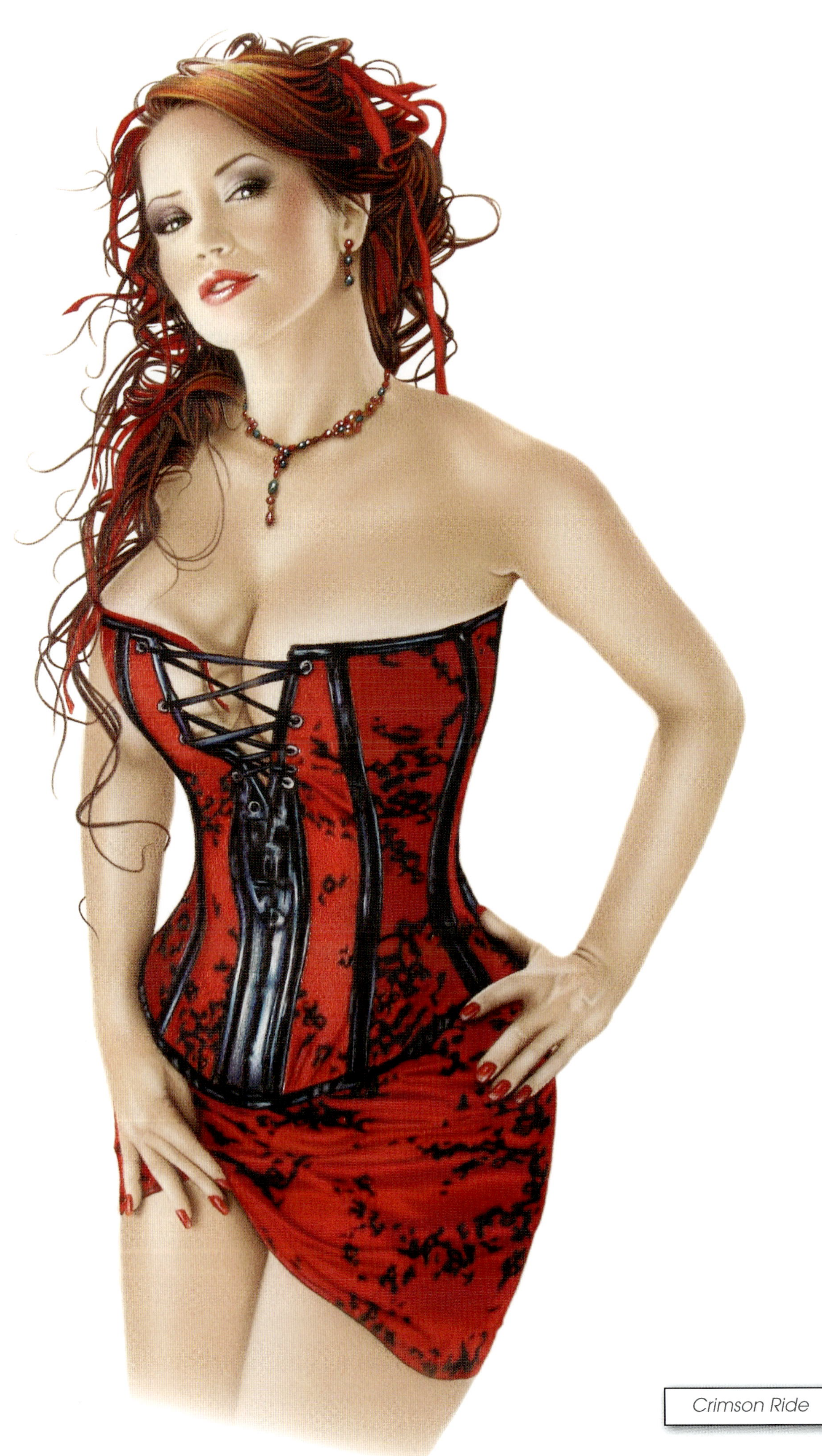

Crimson Ride

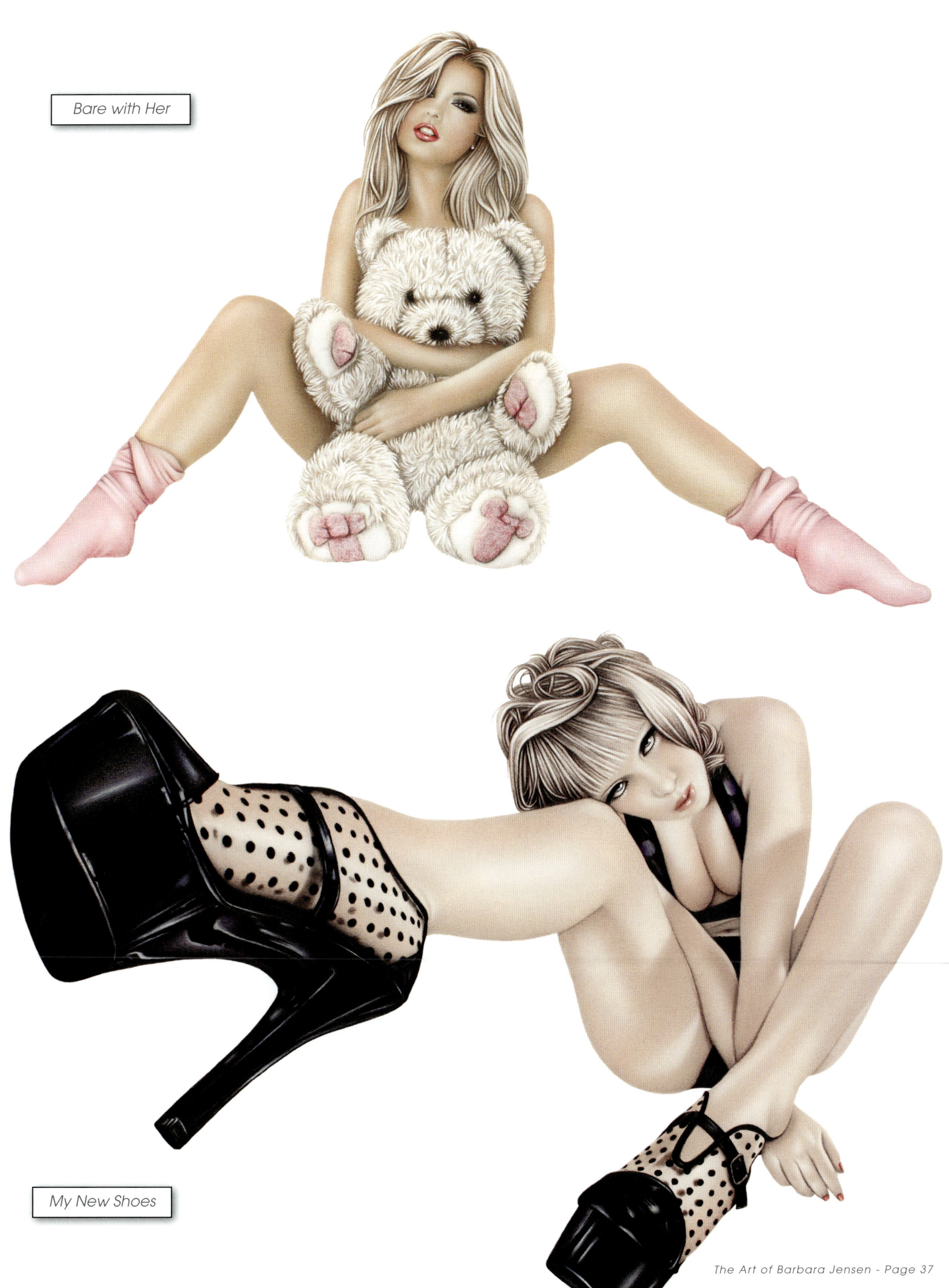

Bare with Her

My New Shoes

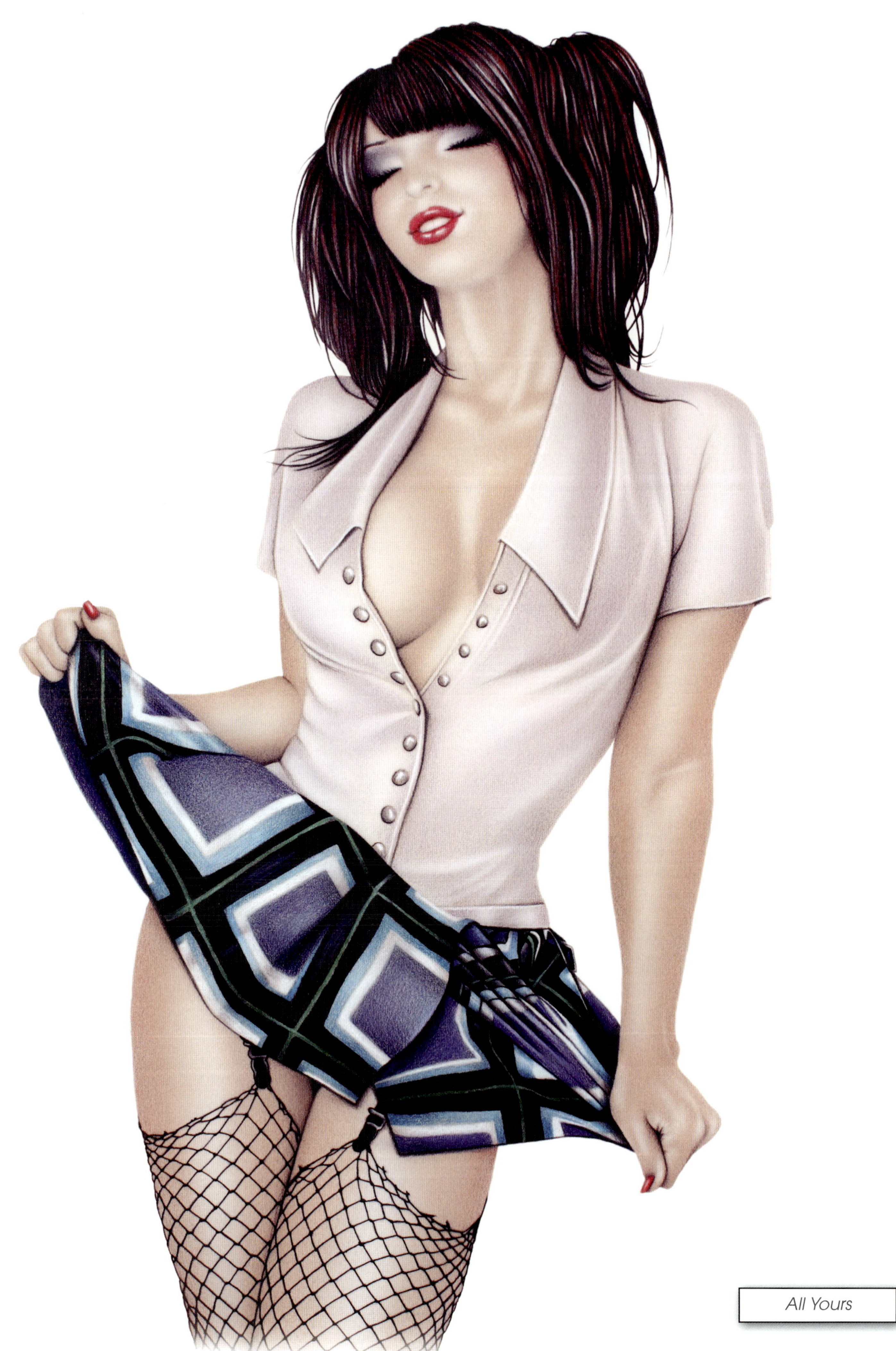

All Yours

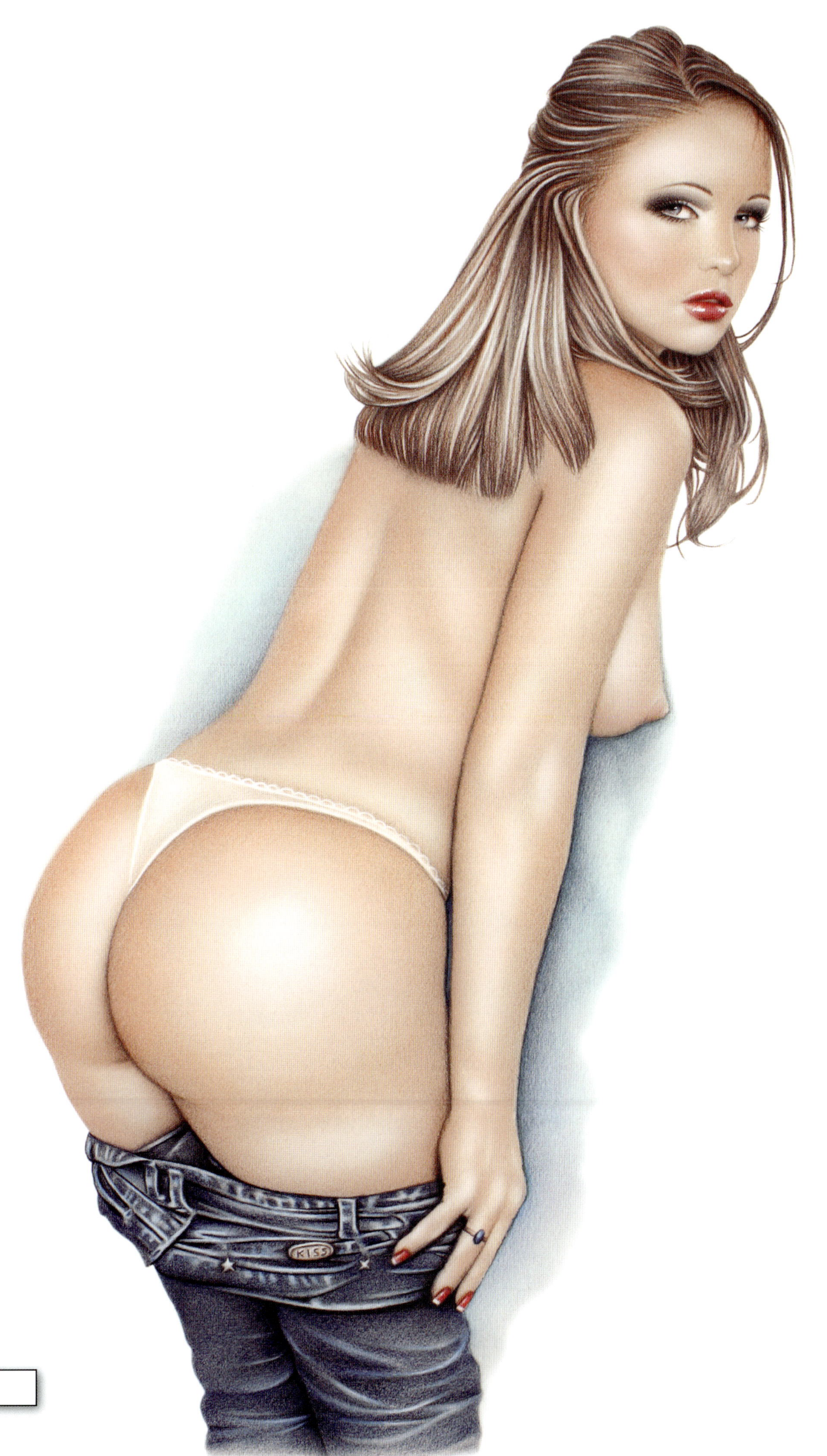

Sweets

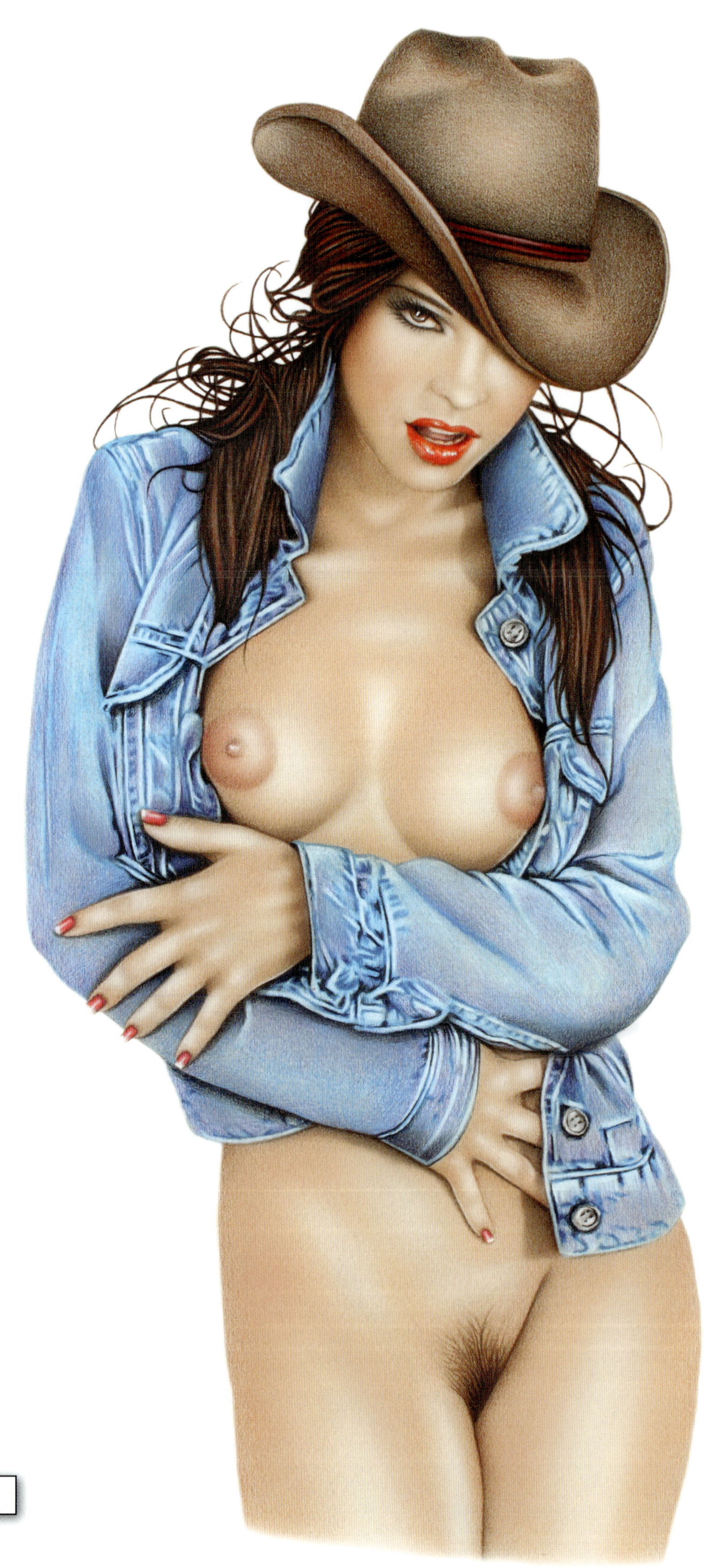

Little Cowgirl

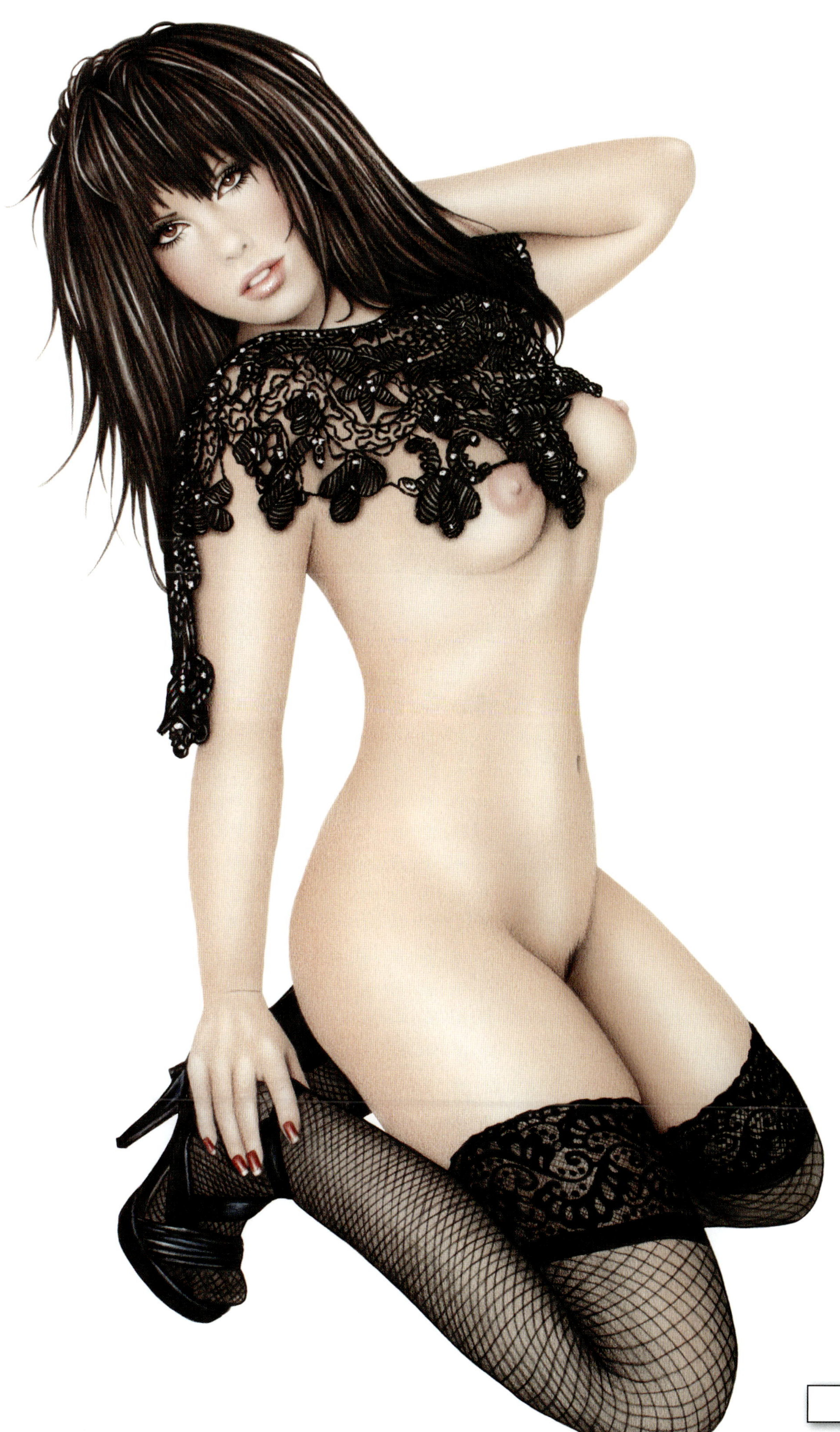

Lyric

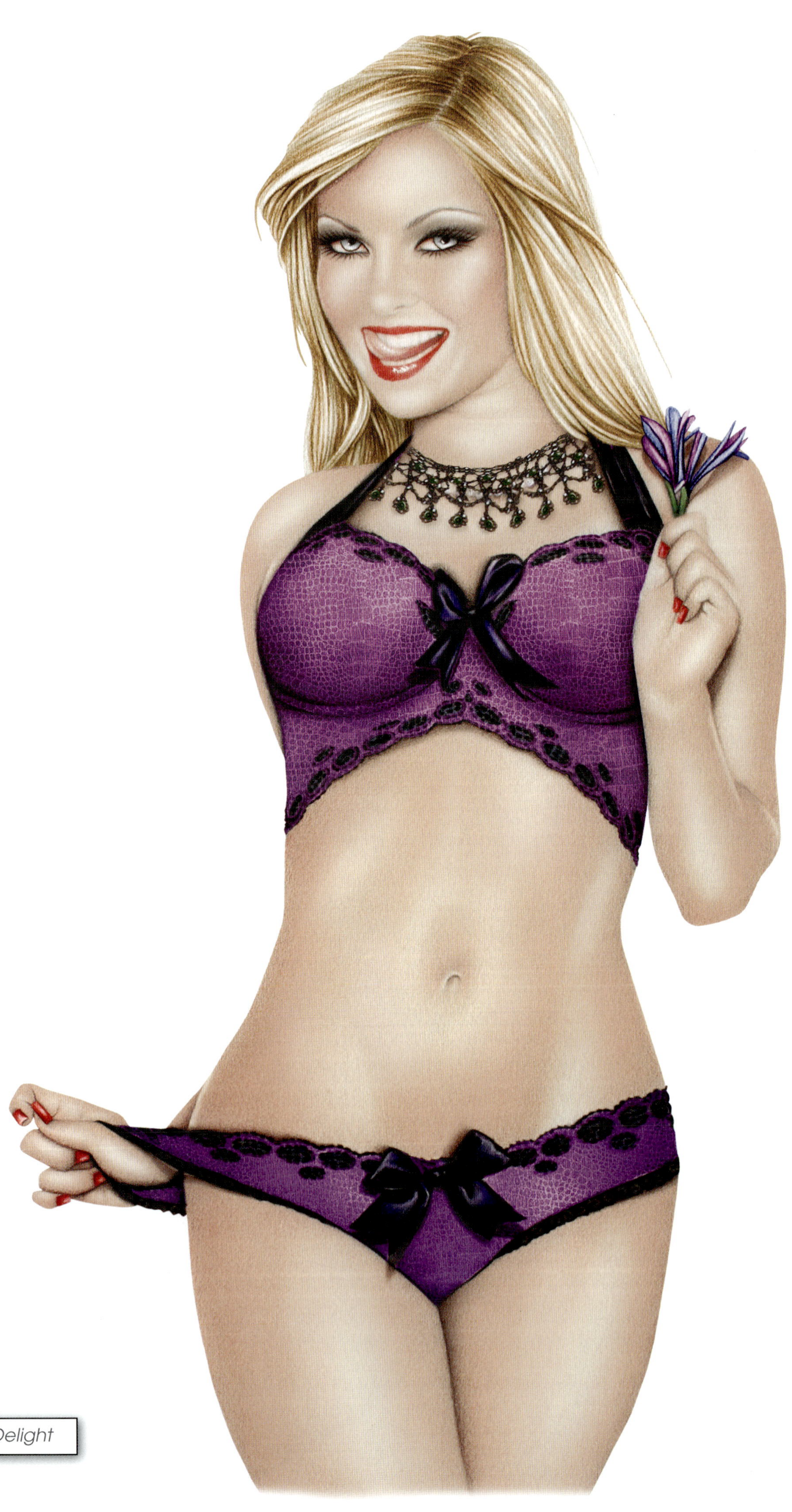

Sheer Delight

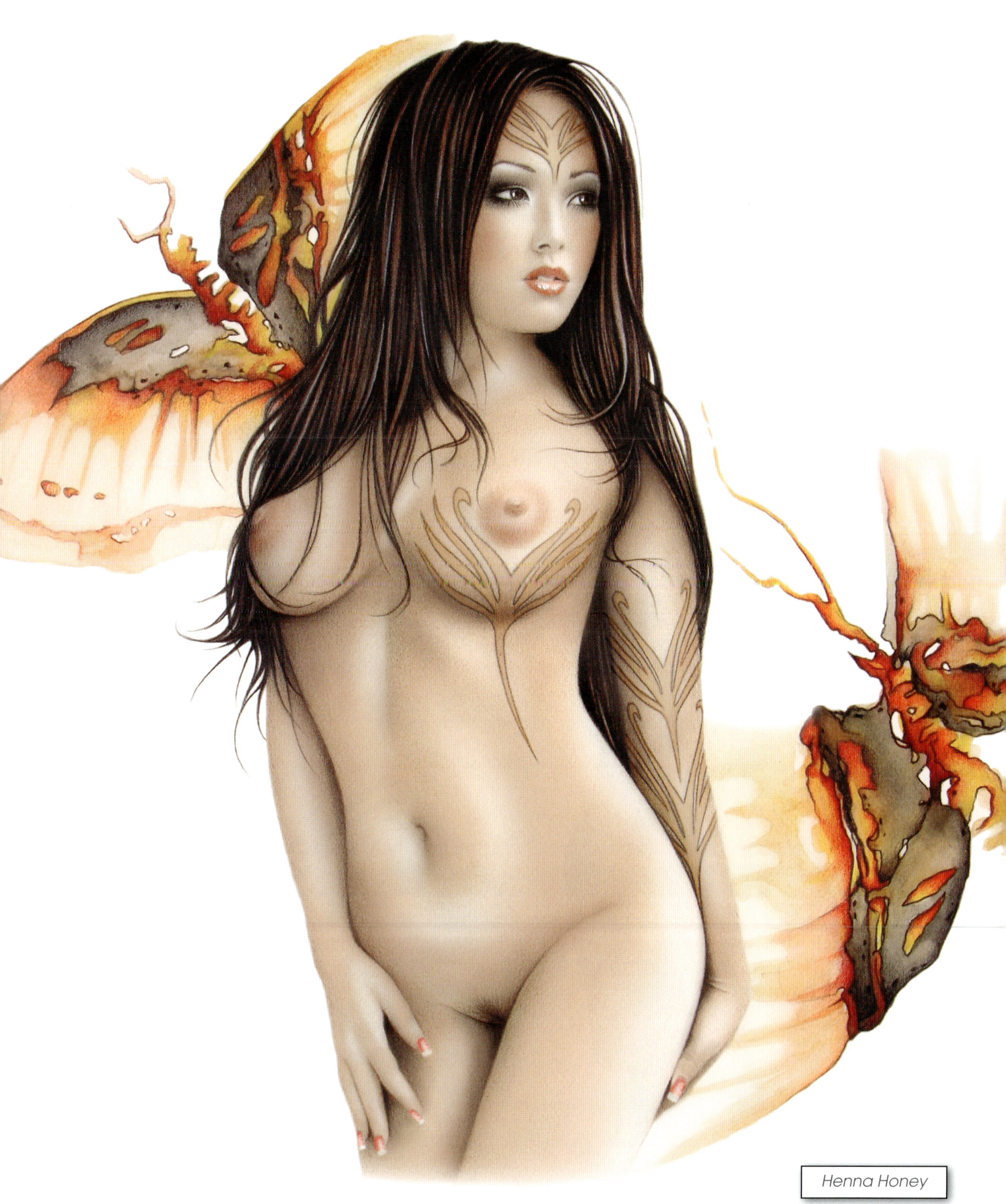

Henna Honey

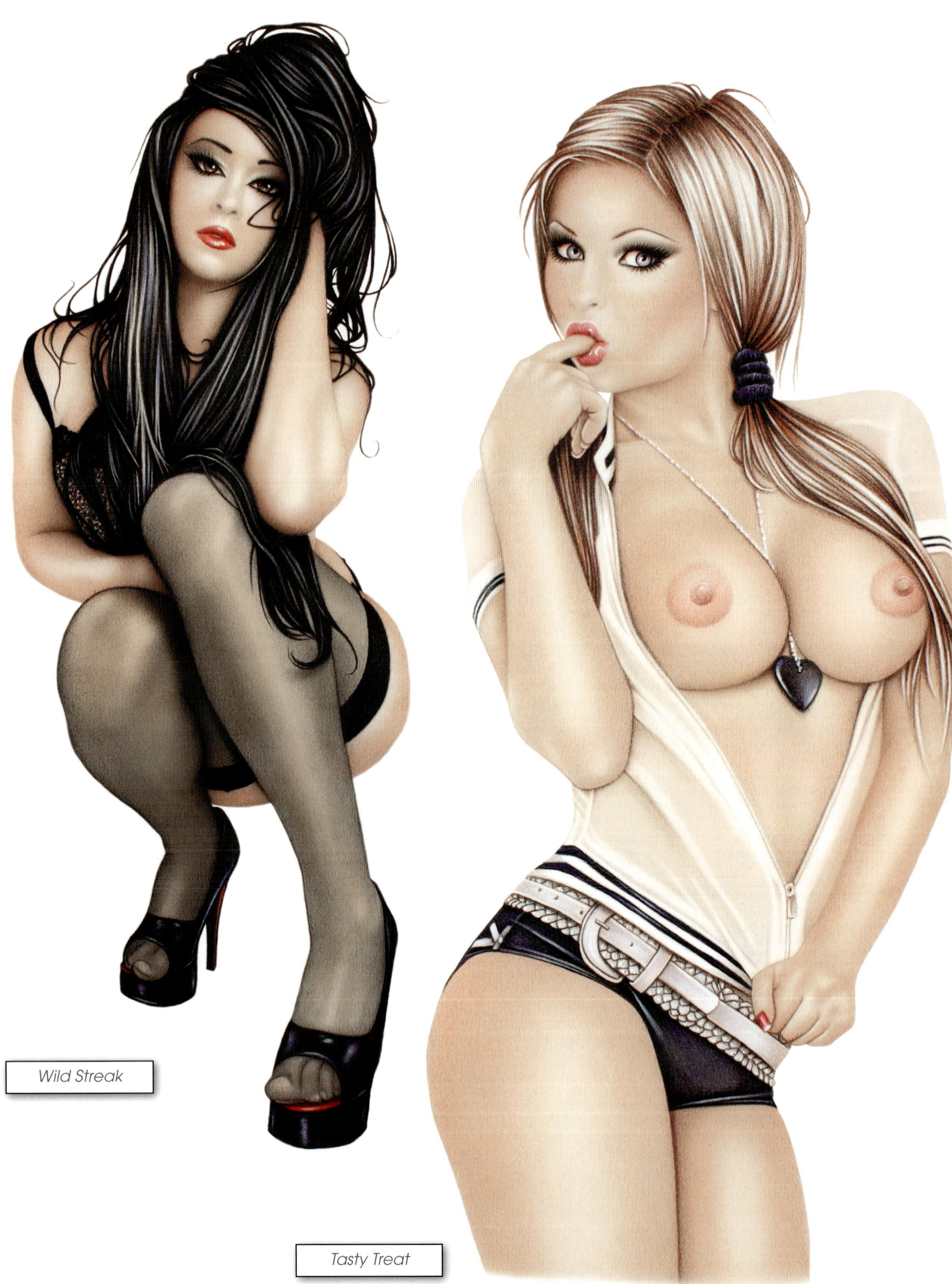

Wild Streak

Tasty Treat

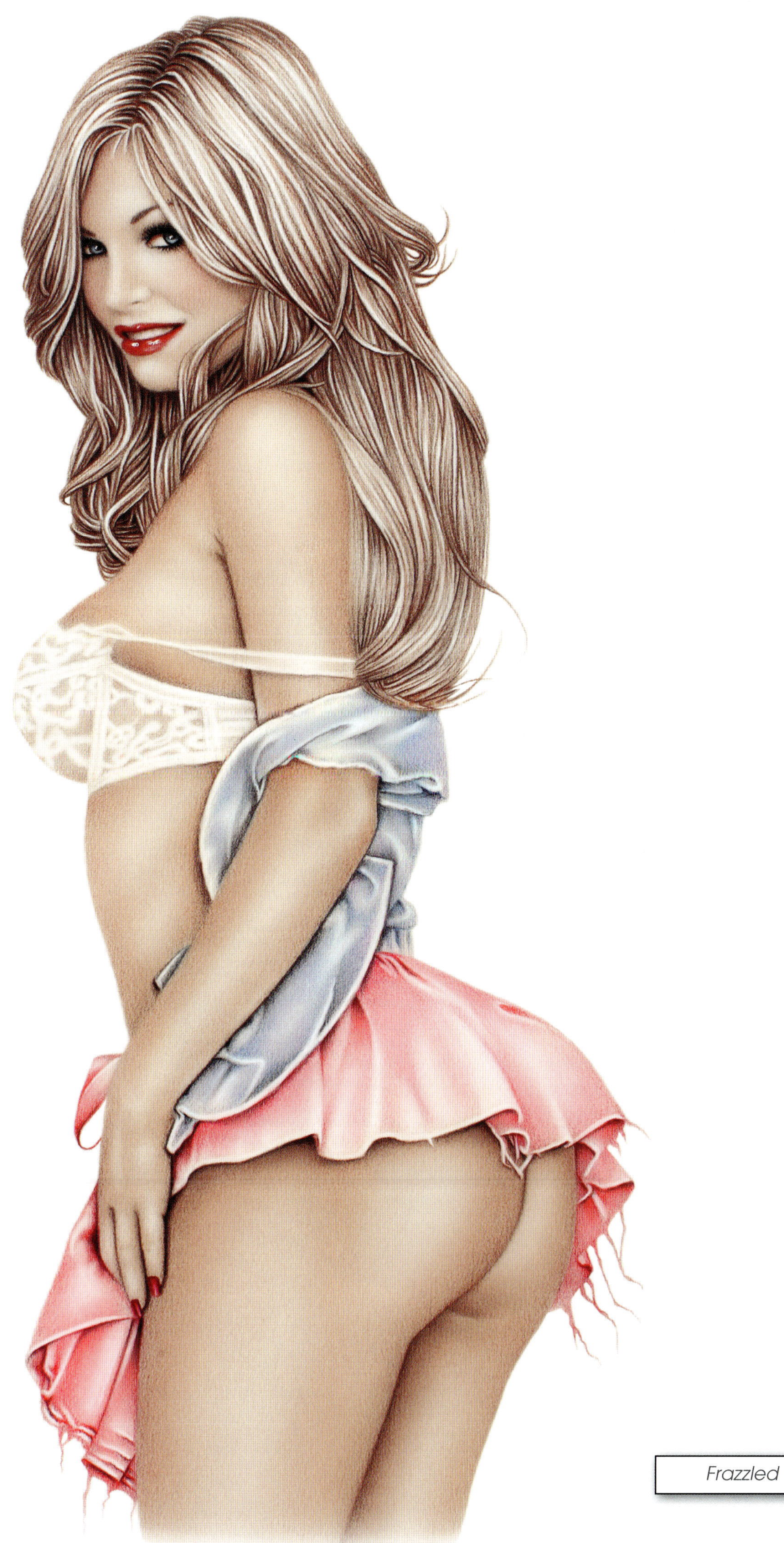

Frazzled

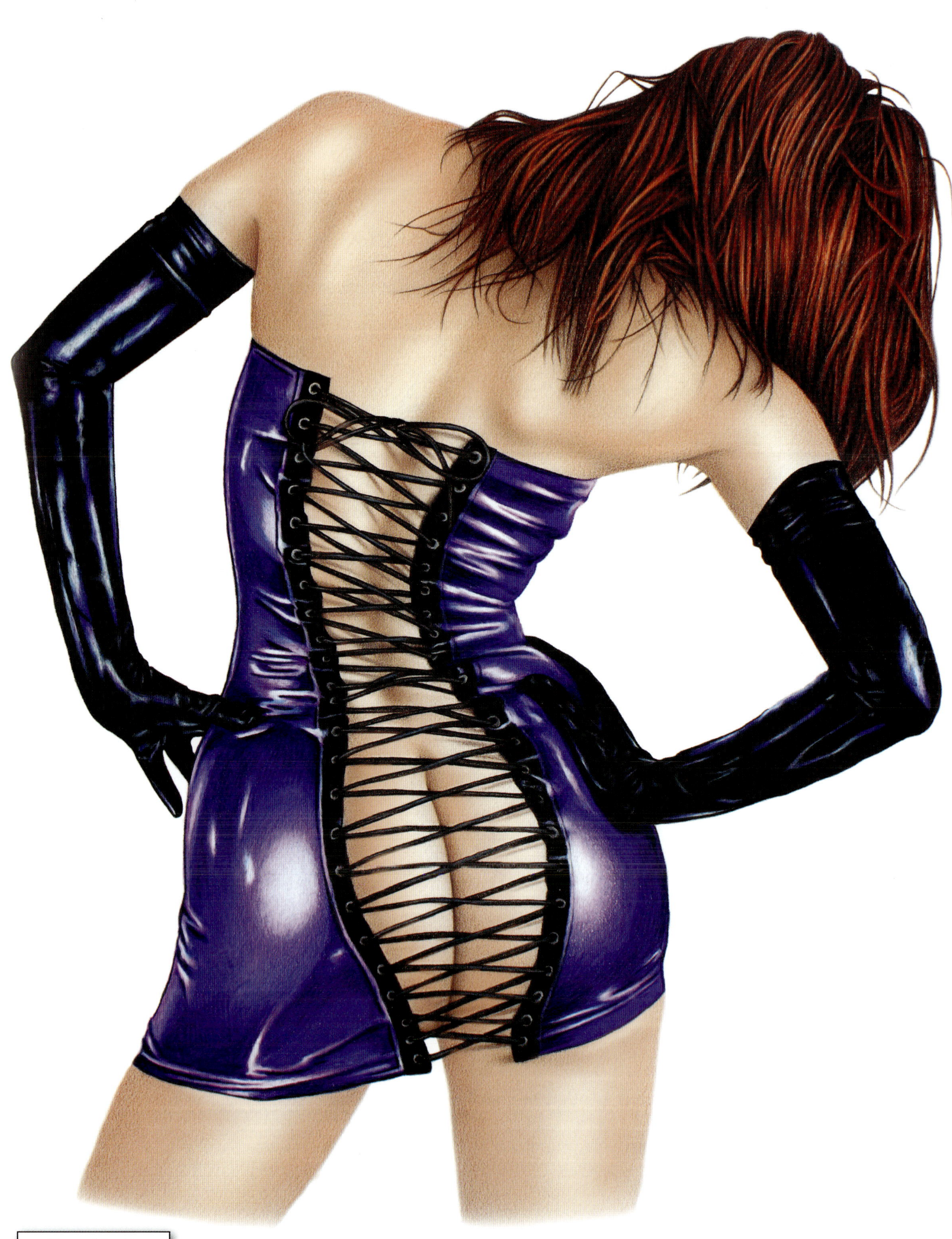

Strap Me Up

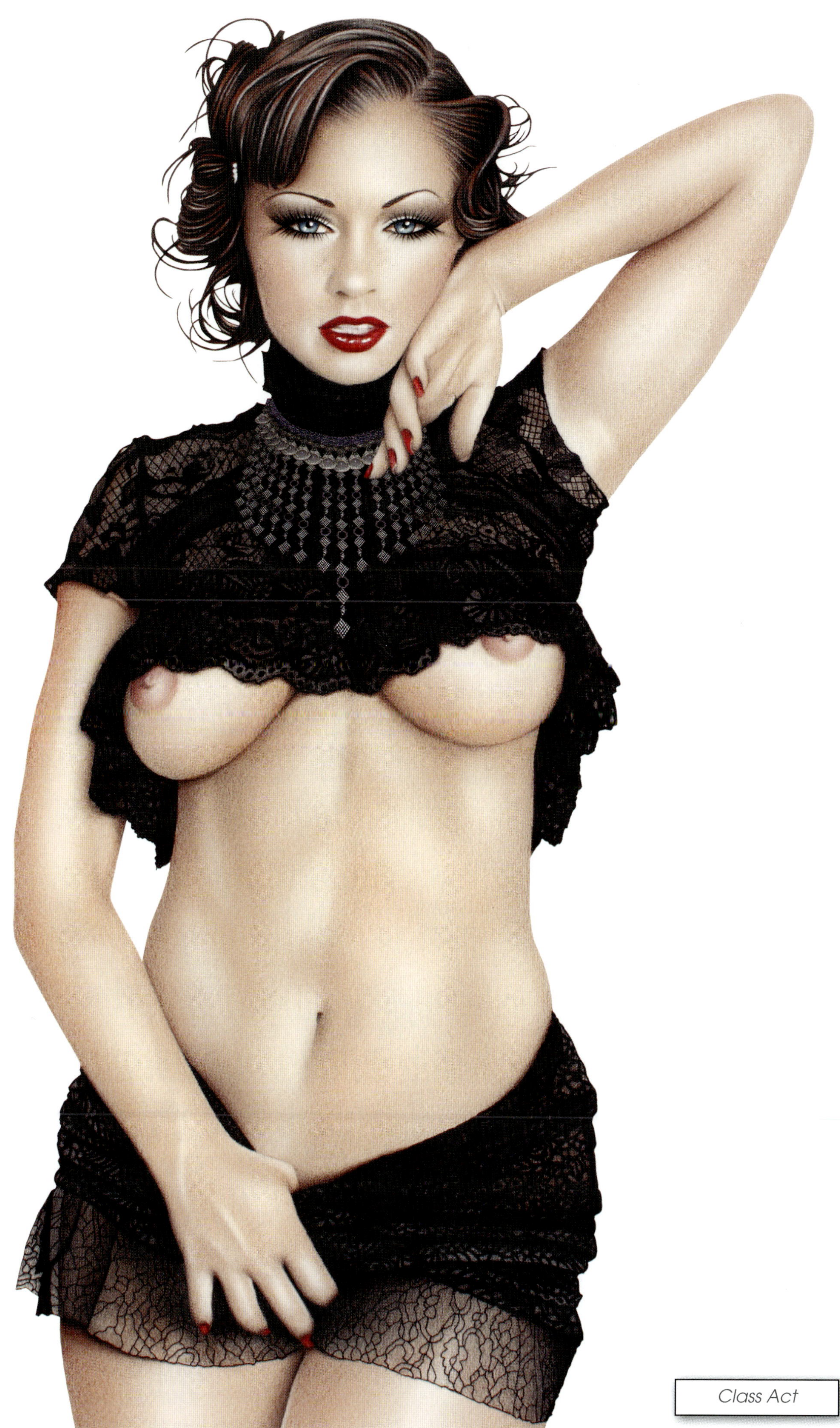

Class Act

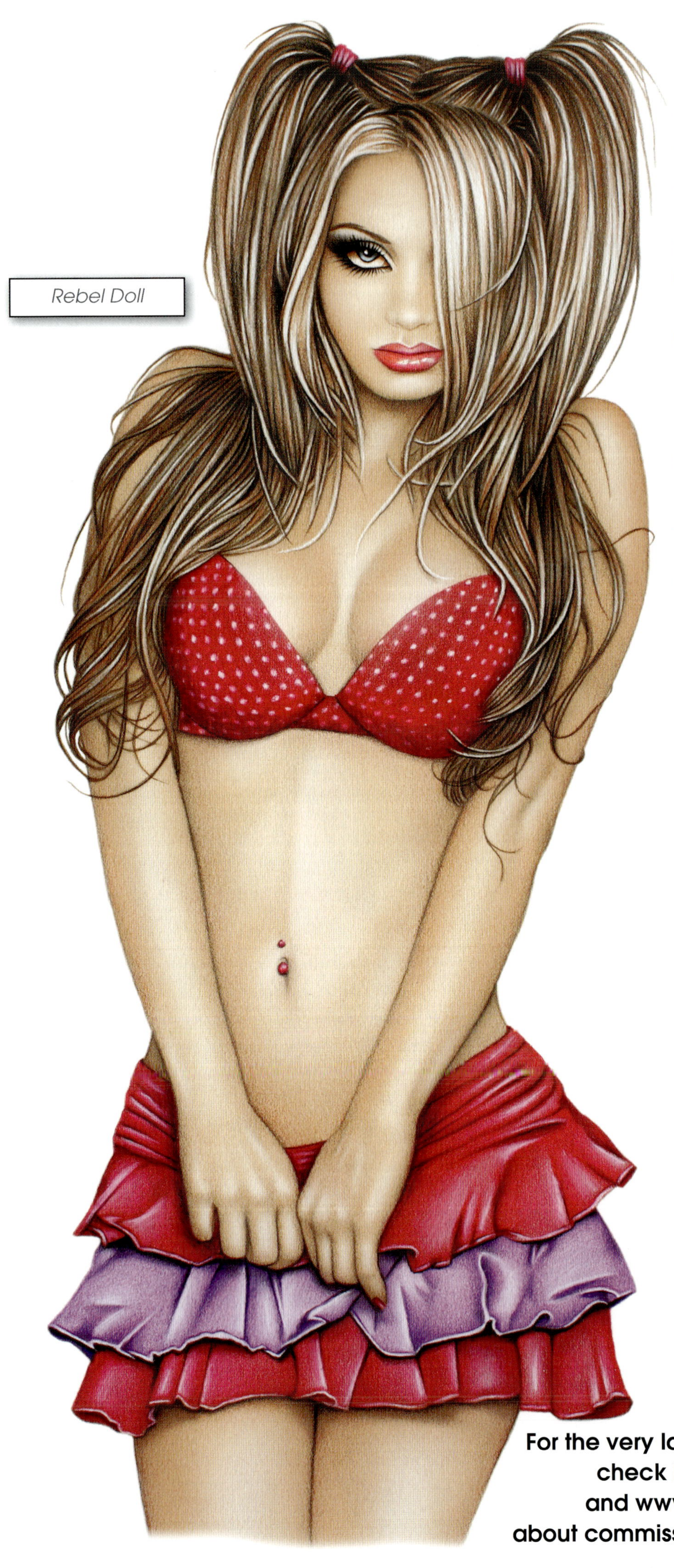

Rebel Doll

I would like to thank all of the models and photographers who have trusted me with their work

Models:

Bianca Beauchamp
www.biancabeauchamp.com
Miss Mosh
www.themoshroom.com
Aria Giovanni
www.ariagiovanni.com
Nicole Moser
www.nicolemoser.com
Zdenka Podkapova
www.sexy-zdenka.com
Charlie Kristine
www.charliekristine.com
Masuimi Max
www.masuimimax.com
Ginger Zero
www.gingerzero.com
Debra A.
Veronica Zemanova
Raven Black
Lyric
Denmark

Photographers:

Suze Randall
www.suze.net
Holly Randall
www.Hollyrandall.com
Dan Richards
http://d2L2.deviantart.com
Martin Perreault
www.martinperreault.com
Rich Cutrone
www.richcutronephotography.com
Jeff Coulter
www.visualpoison.com
David April
www.dsa157.com

For the very latest on what Barbara Jensen is doing, check her out at www.Eroticartistgallery.com and www.Barbarajensentubes.com. To inquire about commissions, write her at Arteest111@aol.com